A Year of Walks in
THE LAKE DISTRICT

Roy Woodcock

Published by Sigma Leisure – an imprint of
Sigma Press, 1 South Oak Lane, Wilmslow, Cheshire SK9 6AR, England.

British Library Cataloguing in Publication Data
A CIP record for this book is available from the British Library.

ISBN: 1-85058-638-1

Typesetting and Design by: Sigma Press, Wilmslow, Cheshire.

Cover photographs, clockwise, from top left: Coniston Old Man from the north-east end of the lake; Red Tarn and Swirral Edge; the cliffs at St Bees; Pike o' Stickle above the Langdale Valley.

Maps: the author
Drawings: Wendy Galassini
Photographs: the author

Printed by: MFP Design and Print

Disclaimer: the information in this book is given in good faith and is believed to be correct at the time of publication. No responsibility is accepted by either the author or publisher for errors or omissions, or for any loss or injury howsoever caused. Only you can judge your own fitness, competence and experience.

Preface

This series of circular walks visits 12 of the outstanding locations in Cumbria and crosses delightful countryside in all of them. The walks are not rugged or arduous, but more for walkers seeking fresh air and exercise, whilst seeing the Lake District in all its moods throughout the year. The choice of walks is inevitably personal, looking for 12 interesting locations, and chosen to show the wide range of features of interest within the Lake District – both for Lake District devotees as well as for the Lake District newcomers. Many famous honey pot locations are visited but it is also shown that even at busy weekends in summer it is possible to find quiet spots in this very busy and popular tourist area, visited by at least 12 million people per annum.

Everywhere in the Lakes is scenically atttractive and the whole area has been designated a National Park. The walks are from 6-11 miles in length and can be taken as a full day out, but there are short cut options of 5-9 miles. This is to enable walkers to have a leisurely half day outing, or a walk to suit families with small children. There are always features of interest on the walks, whether it is a nature reserve with flowers or birds, an old church, the local geology, or links with famous writers.

It is hoped that references to the weather, the landscape and the features of natural history which might be seen or experienced in each month will add to the interest and enjoyment of each walk. The features of natural history mentioned are generally those which are likely to be seen during the walk, not the rare or shy for which a lengthy wait may be required. It is hoped that the walks will enable you to discover features of the landscape which perhaps had not been noticed before, and to appreciate the countryside as it changes through the year. Each month has its own particular attractions, but although the walks specifically refer to a particular month, they can all be enjoyed at any time of the year. The maps and the detailed description of the route will enable anyone to follow these walks without danger of getting lost, although local maps may be useful in providing further information about the areas which are being crossed. Any steep climbs are referred to in the description, as are any locations which might be available for refreshment.

Routes were all correct when last walked, which was during 1998. The weather comments included with each walk contain both the general or average for the month, but also specific to the region and to the particular year this was written. Countryside comments are also both specific and general, general to the month and the region, but with occasional more specific comments only relevant to the walk being described.

Acknowledgements

I am grateful for the advice and encouragement from Michael Robinson and all the comfortable days spent at his Burn How Garden House Hotel in Bowness. My thanks also to the National Park Authority at Brock Hole for providing useful information and to Alistair Crowle at the RSPB North of England Office for replying to my enquires and requests for answers to specific questions. Thanks once again to Wendy for her delightful drawings which enhance the appearance of this book, and biggest thanks of all to Margaret for accompanying me on these walks and then spending many hours checking and advising on the text.

All the walks can be found on the Outdoor Leisure 1:25,000 maps of the English Lakes, numbers 4, 5, 6 and 7, with the exception of the May walk which is on the older Pathfinder series number 593.

Roy Woodcock

Contents

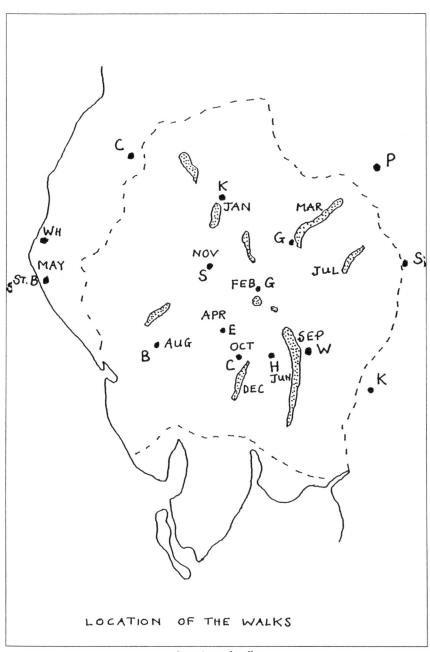

LOCATION OF THE WALKS

Locations of walks

Introduction

The Lake District is a small, compact, almost circular area within the county of Cumbria, and extends no more than 30 miles from north to south or west to east. The County covers an area of 682,451 hectares (the second largest county in England) and has a population of nearly half a million (one of the smallest of any county).

The Lake District extends from Kendal in the south to Keswick and Cockermouth in the north, and from Shap in the east to Wastwater and Ennerdale in the west. The only main roads to cross this region are the A591 from Kendal to Keswick and A66 from Cockermouth to Penrith. The A590 and A595 run along the southern and western coasts, and the A6 and M6 fringe the eastern margins.

Geology

Geology has influenced much of the scenery and many of the rocks date from 500 million years ago. Three groups of rocks make up the main part of the Lake District, and from south to north these are the Silurian shales, the Borrowdale volcanics and the Skiddaw slates. These old rocks were covered by younger rocks in the Carboniferous period and then the whole area was uplifted by the Hercynian earth movements about 290 million years ago. After that time, desert conditions prevailed in the Permian and Triassic geological periods, known as the New Red Sandstone time. This was about 250 million years ago, and desert sands were laid down around the edges of the mountains. The high ground was dome-shaped, and rivers flowed out from the centre in all directions, like the spokes of a wheel. This saw the creation of the radial pattern, which was followed by glaciers and which can be seen in the present-day valleys.

The continuous processes of erosion removed the Carboniferous rocks from the top of the dome and so the older rocks have been exposed in the main part of the Lake District, with the younger Carboniferous limestones and Coal Measures as well as the New Red Sandstones found around the edges. Limestone of Carboniferous age is seen on the southern margins of the lakes and Coal Measures,

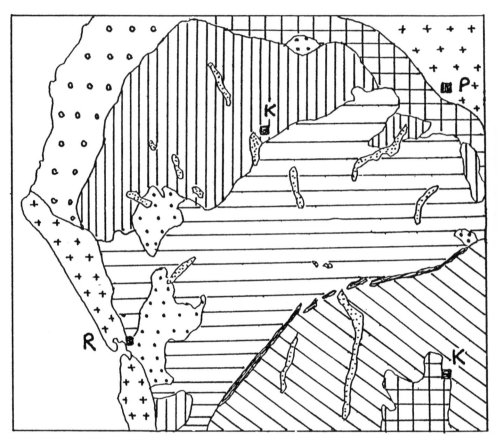

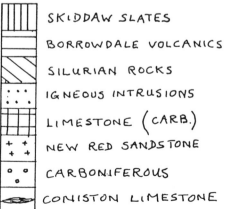

SKIDDAW SLATES

BORROWDALE VOLCANICS

SILURIAN ROCKS

IGNEOUS INTRUSIONS

LIMESTONE (CARB.)

NEW RED SANDSTONE

CARBONIFEROUS

CONISTON LIMESTONE

Simplified geological map of the Lake District

also of Carboniferous age, have been found near Workington and Whitehaven. The younger sandstones of Permian age are seen near Barrow, St Bees and in the Eden Valley.

The old rocks, which really make up the main part of the Lake District, belong to three geological groups. The youngest are the Silurian shales and sands, about 430 million years old, and formed when this area was covered by an ocean. These are to be seen near Windermere and Coniston (see map on facing page), and to the north of these rocks are the Borrowdale Volcanics which include the Langdale Valley, Helvellyn and Scafell. These rocks are mainly basalts or andesites and resulted from violent volcanic activity about 450 million years ago, in the later part of the Ordovician period. They often weather into crags and cliffs. The northern Lakes around Keswick are made up of the Skiddaw series of rocks, mudstones and sandstones laid down in an ocean, and date from the early part of the Ordovician period, about 500 million years ago. These often weather to form smooth and rounded surfaces. Forcing up through these three regions are the igneous intrusions which formed about 400 million years ago and can be seen in the granites of Shap in the east, and Eskdale in the west.

All these rocks have been eroded for millions of years, and then there have been several advances and retreats of the ice during the last two million years. Advancing ice has enlarged river valleys to form the large U-shaped valleys and has also gouged out hollows which have been filled with water to form ribbon lakes. Glacial retreat has been associated with melting ice and the deposition of material to fill in hollows, leave ridges of morainic material and elongated mounds called drumlins. In the last 12,000 years since the Ice Age, some of the mounds have been worn down, and the hollows have been filled. All the numerous lakes, whether large and long, or small and more circular are now being filled up by deposits carried by rivers flowing into the lakes. It can be seen in Derwent Water (January walk), or Easedale Tarn (February walk) where deltaic deposition is taking place, when the rivers flow into lakes, slow down and lose carrying power, so being forced to deposit some of their sediment.

The geomorphology (shape of the landscape) is the result of the geological structure and the way the various rocks have been changed with time and with erosion. Many of the features of landscape are the direct result of ice action, but others are determined more by the geological history, or the structural form, or the rock type, and it is a combination of these influences which has created the wonderful scenery which exists today. A few features of the local geomorphology are included in each walk, either in the Countryside section or where encountered on the walk.

Early man

Not much is known of the early inhabitants of the Lake District who first settled here and who gave it many of the names. Stone circles are evidence of the earliest residents, and possibly they were searching for minerals. Neolithic man began clearing the forests from the hillsides to create farming land. The Romans created a port at Ravenglass, and built a major fort at Hardknott Pass (August walk). They used the ridge called High Street (July walk) as one of their major through routes, on the way to and from Hadrians Wall. Northumbrian people came into the area and farmed, and were followed by the Norse who arrived via Ireland and the Isle of Man in the 8th and 9th centuries. They were mainly pastoralists, and cleared many woodlands and created farms.

Place names

Many of the large lakes are called meres, e.g. Windermere, Grasmere, and some of the smaller lakes are called tarns. These names e.g. mere have been derived from Old English (mere means a lake) and others are Norse (Scandinavian) words (tarn = tear drop). Other names of Scandinavian origin include beck (a brook or stream), fell (a hill), gill (deep valley or ravine), rigg (a ridge) thwaite (a clearing). Langdale means a long valley. Several other references to the origin of place names are made in the individual walks.

National Park

The National Park was designated in 1951, and covers an area of 2,292 sq.km. (885 sq.mls.). Most of it is now classified as Environmentally Sensitive Areas. The total population of the Park area is about 42,000 and about one third of these people are dependent on tourism.

The Lake District National Park is entirely within Cumbria and includes the hilly area with the large lakes, which give the area its name. Excluded from the National Park are the lowland areas along the southern coast of Cumbria, near Morecambe Bay, the west coastal region and the coast along the Solway Firth in the north. Cumbria contains many beautiful stretches of coastline, though these are not inside the National Park, and also excluded from the National Park is the low-lying part of Cumbria along the Eden Valley in the north east.

The aims of the National Park Authority are: to conserve the natural beauty, wildlife and cultural heritage of the Lake District; to pro-

mote opportunities for enjoyment and understanding of the National Park; and foster the interests of the local community. Tourism is now a very important part of Lake District life, and as we take something by the pleasure derived from a visit, we should also contribute by spending a little money in the area, making use of local shops or cafes.

The National Trust owns nearly 25% (52,778 ha) of the Lake District, and nearly 60% is privately owned. The remainder is owned by North West Water, the Forestry Commission, the National Park Authority (only 3.8%) and the Ministry of Defence.

Weather

The Lake District is noted for its weather, and not always in a favourable light. It is certainly wet, one of the wettest parts of England because of its location in the north and west of the country, and also because it contains high ground which attracts the cloud and rain. The weather systems bringing the rain are generally the fast moving westerlies, and so bright weather can often appear quickly even on the wettest of days.

Weather is important to walkers, and nowhere more so than in the Lake District, and it would be foolish to venture out on a walk without appropriate weatherproof clothing. The wind and rain are able to penetrate most types of clothing and it is certainly wise to obtain good quality rainproof gear. Many shops in the Lake District are only too keen to sell you some, and can generally offer sound advice about your purchases. At higher levels the weather is much wetter than in the valleys, so even if it is fine down near the roads, the weather conditions on the hills can be quite different, and throughout much of the year can become almost like the Arctic. Temperature decrease and wind chill are also serious factors at higher level.

Factual weather information

Temperatures

Temperatures decrease with height, which is why it is colder up on the fells than in the valleys – even though you may become very warm whilst walking uphill – do not be fooled by this! The rate of decrease is about 0.6° C per 100 metres. Carlisle averages 4°C in January and 15 in July, but the lowest recorded temperature was minus 21° at Ambleside in January 1940.

About 40 air frosts are recorded annually in the lowlands, and around 80 ground frosts with figures of 150 and 170 respectively being recorded on the peaks. Frost is most likely during settled anticyclonic weather, and in these conditions mist may accumulate in the valleys or over the lakes, as the cold air rolls down the hillsides into the valley bottoms.

Sunshine

Carlisle records an annual average total of 1393 hours of sunshine, with the lowest totals of 47-48 hours in December and January, with 183 and 191 hours in the two sunniest months of May and June. The coastal plain of Cumbria averages 1500 hours of sunshine, Keswick averages 1270 hours and the hill tops a total of 1000 hours. But ... the area is more famous for rainfall!

Rainfall

Rainfall is generally over 1200mm in the hilly areas, with 4000+ in the Scafell-Great Gable area. The annual total is down to 800mms in the rain shadow area of the Eden Valley, with 900-1000mm along the coastal plain. In the hilly areas there are remarkable variations in very short distances.

Carlisle averages 834mm per annum, with 45mm the average in April, the driest month, and 87mm in September, the wettest month. The range of rainfall totals elsewhere in the Lake District can be clearly seen by the following figures.

Sprinkling Tarn, at 600 metres above sea level, records 4298mm in an average year, with March to June the driest months, but still over 250mm each month.

Seathwaite, at 107 metres, receives 3300mm per annum.

A mile away at Rosthwaite, height 101 metres, the annual average is 2469mm, and at Keswick (77m) the total is 1496mm A few miles further east, Penrith (149m) averages 868mm.

Snowfall

The total number of days with falling snow or sleet recorded, increase by 5 for every 100 metres of height gained. Snow rarely lies on low ground before November or after the end of March, but at higher levels snow may be seen any time from October till May. Lying snow is recorded on 12-15 days in Ambleside, 5-10 at Carlisle (with up to 30 days recording falling snow or sleet) and over 60 on the hills. The days of snow cover recorded on Helvellyn over a period of years are: December 2, January 13, February 29, March 9, April 5.

BUT ...

In spite of all that gloom and doom there are many good days and parts of days. One sunny day makes you forget the rainy days which have gone before, or on a rainy day when the sun makes a belated appearance, the views will often be amazing, walking will be exhilarating and inspiration may encourage you to write poetry, as happened to Wordsworth and his friends.

In his "Morning after a storm", William Wordsworth wrote:

> *There was a roaring in the wind all night*
> *The rain came heavily and fell in floods*
> *But now the sun is rising calm and bright.*

Much has been made of the links with the great poets, and a high degree of commercialisation has taken place in the Lake District, for which it has received criticism. However the Lake District is not a museum, and many people can earn a living in the area, thanks not only to the beautiful scenery but also as a result of this commercialisation.

Advisory

Each walk is accompanied by a map and together with the detailed description of the walk this should enable anyone to find and follow the route. However it will be useful to have the 1:25,000 Outdoor Leisure (or perhaps the 1:50,000 Landranger maps) in case of problems with the route and also to provide information and detail about the surrounding area. It is always advisable to carry a compass, which can be especially useful on bare hills, in woodlands or in fog, when sense of direction may be lost.

Many places will be muddy, especially in winter, and some sections of the walks are steep or stony. Therefore boots are advisable. It is also advisable, or even essential, to carry windproof and waterproof clothing, as well as a warm drink and some food if going out all day, even though there are locations for refreshment on most of the walks described.

Binoculars are very handy, especially if you are at all interested in bird life, and they sometimes help to pinpoint the location of stiles at the opposite side of large fields. Cameras too are useful, as all the walks contain many photogenic locations.

All details were correct at the time of walking (in 1998). All the walks follow public rights of way, and were free from obstructions at the time of last walking the routes described.

January

Keswick area

The hills at Castlerigg and Walla Crag are the two ascents on this circular walk from Keswick, and the final miles are alongside the lake shore. Throughout the walk magnificent scenery can be seen in all directions though Walla Crag provides the most memorable views. The descent from Walla passes Ashness Bridge, one of the most famous of all Lakeland features – and rightly so as you will see when you get there.

Length: 8 miles, with two possible short cuts if required.

Time required: 4-5 hours.

Terrain: undulating with one steep climb, and a very gentle final two miles alongside the lake.

Map: 1:25,000 O.S. Outdoor Leisure map 4, The English Lakes, North Western Area

Starting point: at the main car park in Keswick, grid ref. 266234. Keswick is reached along the A591 from Windermere or A66 from Penrith. Bus services link the neighbouring towns, but there is no railway line (though there is a station).

Facilities: Tourist Information Centre: in the town centre (017687 72645). Wide variety of refreshments available in Keswick.

Weather

As in the rest of England, the Lake District often experiences spells of mild westerly weather even in January, but there can be spells of bitterly cold weather, especially when the wind, and the weather, is coming from the east or north. The mild westerlies will bring rain in large quantities, and it is well known that Seathwaite has a weather station which is generally the wettest in England. The rainfall has been measured here since 1840 and the average is about 3300mm per annum, compared with 1000-1200mm on the coastal lowlands not many miles away. There are undoubtedly wetter places than Seathwaite in the Lake District and in other hilly areas of Wales and Scotland, but there are no long term records to give a precise figure. A few readings show that the higher parts of Scafell or Great Gable are wetter than down in the valley near Seathwaite. Dry weather in January is likely to be cold and possibly snowy, which can change the entire appearance of the Lake District. 1998 was a very mild month for the first half, but after that, there were a few days with a maximum temperature of only 2 or 3°. There was only a light covering of snow which lasted for a few days. The outstanding memory of the weather was the rain, associated with the mild weather, and the rivers were full and the grass remained green and useful as a food for the sheep. The old saying: *'If the grass grows in Janiveer, It grows the wuss for it all the year'*, is based on the gloomy prediction that we will pay for it later, but the long term records do not support this viewpoint.

The countryside

The appearance of the landscape will be strongly influenced by the weather and the amount of snow cover, which can make the hills look very Alpine. The higher parts are often snow covered for a week or two, but the valleys and the roads are rarely affected for more than one or two days. The rivers are often flowing fast and can cause floods though these are less serious than in the past, as many of the main channels have been built up and strengthened. However, the fields and hillsides become very wet at this time of year, with no warm sunshine to evaporate any of the

Heron

moisture. In the valley the fields are mainly in pasture, and may contain a few beef cattle and the hardy sheep, although the sheep are often left on the hillsides unless the weather becomes very severe. The hillsides tend to look dull and brownish with the winter vegetation, but there are rich green areas too, especially where the water loving plants are growing. When walking on the hills, it is useful to be able to recognise the mosses and grasses growing in very damp environments, in order to avoid them whenever possible. Few flowers will be seen at this time of year, although snowdrops will be growing well in any mild spells. The broad-leaved deciduous trees will be bare, and the coniferous woods will be looking very dark, except where there are stands of larch, which give a different shade, as their needles will have dropped. Bird life is also quite scarce in winter, but there are the usual common birds near the houses in the valleys, and winter visitors such as redwings and fieldfares, with a few snow buntings up on the fells. Gulls, ducks and geese can be seen searching for food in the lakes.

The landscape has been strongly influenced through millennia by the geology and the type of rocks, but in more recent times by the activity of the ice. Descending from Walla Crag down into the deep valley shows the power of glacial erosion, but whilst walking along the lakeside, many effects of glacial deposition will be seen. During the period known as the Devensian to Geologists, about 30,000-15,000 years ago, ice covered the Lake District for the last time. Deposits of rock debris were laid down as the ice melted, and elongated mounds of rocks and clay are known as drumlins; examples can be seen in Crow Park, Friars Crag and the Stable Hills.

Keswick

Often regarded as the capital of the northern lakes, this small town is a very popular tourist centre, and its well stocked Tourist Information Centre is situated along the main street, in the old Moot Hall which dates from 1813. Keswick has attracted many artists and poets, and in the past it was home to both Southey and Coleridge. There have been ancient links with mining in nearby hills, and pencils have been made here since the 16th century, originally using local graphite. The pencil factory now has a museum open throughout the year, showing the history of graphite mining and celebrating the fact that this was the location of the world's first pencils. The parish church of St John Evangelist is not built of local stone, but of soft and easily carved sandstone from the Eden Valley. It was built in the 1830s in Old English style, and originally consisted of the tower and spire and the central part of the nave and vestry. Extensions were added in 1862 (a north aisle) and 1889 (the chancel). One of the outstanding features is the east window, which dates from 1879, though it was taken out and replaced later, whilst the chancel was being added. The views from the churchyard are spectacular.

Derwent Water

Often called "The Queen of the Lakes", this long narrow lake is called a ribbon or finger lake by geomorphologists. It is situated in a hollow which was dug out by a glacier, and the small islands in the lake may be formed where harder lumps of rock have not been eroded, though some are drumlins, mounds of glacial debris deposited by ice as it melted. The lake was probably much longer and joined to Bassenthwaite in the past. The land which now separates these two lakes is mostly deltaic in origin, deposited by the River Greta and other small streams. Keswick has grown on this low lying ground. The lake is surrounded by hills, generally more rounded in the north where the rocks are the Skiddaw slates (about 500 million

Goosander on Derwent Water

years old and formed in the late Cambrian and early Ordovician Geological periods), but more rugged in the south and east where the harder Borrowdale Volcanics (about 450 million years old and formed during violent volcanic activity in the Ordovician period) are the main rocks. The west side of the lake is dominated by Cat Bells, at the foot of which is Brandelhow, the first land owned by the National Trust in the Lake District, acquired in 1902 through the efforts of Canon Rawnsley. Boat trips or hiring small boats are popular activities on this lake.

Castlerigg Stone Circle

One of the best of the 40 stone circles in Cumbria, these stones are surrounded by hills in all directions, Blencathra and Skiddaw to the north and the Helvellyn mass to the south east. Walla Crag, the route of our walk is to the south west. It is possible that Keats wrote about the fallen Titans in *Hyperion* after his visit to Castlerigg in 1881:

.........like a dismal cirque
Of Druid stones, upon a forlorn moor,

The National Trust has owned the field and stones since 1913, and provide useful information boards at the entrances. There are 38 stones in the circle, 33 of which are still standing, and ten extra stones make up a small rectangle inside the circle. They are all fairly local stones, glacial erratics deposited in this area by the melting ice. The circle was probably constructed about 5000 years ago, though little is known of its history, as few relics have been unearthed. Three stone axes found in the circle may suggest that trading of axes took place here during Neolithic times. Whatever its history, it is a dramatic and impressive monument set on this small hilltop above Keswick.

Derwent Island

This small island has been owned by the National Trust since 1951, and the small stately home is looked after by tenants who are also custodians of the property. The 18th century house is a magnificent lakeland stone building, but is not an easy place to live in or look after, because of its insular location. There is generally no access for the public, though the house is officially open on five days each year. Occasionally strong winds make it impossible to get to or from the island, and some winters the lake freezes which again makes it impossible to use the boat.

The Walk

Leave the main car park in the town (1), and walk along the A5271 signposted to Windermere. Pass Southey Street and Wordsworth Street on the right, and the River Greta on the left. Where the old railway bridge crosses the road, a footpath goes right, following this old line, and can be reached through the garage if you wish to get off the road. Otherwise, keep straight ahead, with the attractive river compensating for the traffic noise, likely to accompany us, even in January.

Go up the hill to leave the town, passing over a railway bridge, with the footpath underneath, to be rejoined by anyone using this alternative route. Keep going up hill and where the Windermere road (A591) turns right, keep straight ahead following signs to

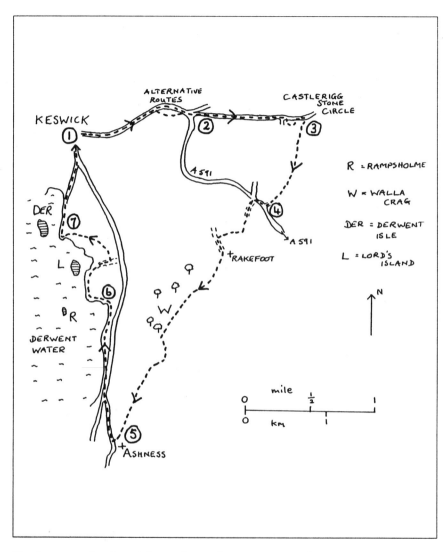

Cockermouth, Penrith and – of more immediate concern – the Castlerigg Stone Circle.

After about 80m, turn right **(2)** along the narrow road to Castlerigg, and walk along this for just over half a mile. Keep climbing steadily, and look out for the old tree stump on the right, with the kind message of "Rest your bones on the way to the stones." A view left will open out to the forests on the lower slopes of Skiddaw (931 metres = 3054 ft, and one of only three Lake District peaks which exceed 3000 feet), and the Blencathra mass further ahead to the left. The main road is down to our left.

A narrow road turns off to the right, and just beyond this are parking spaces, and on the right is the stone circle, on a prominent hill, with good views all around.

Back on the road, and going on beyond the stones, as the road begins to descend slightly, turn right through a gate **(3)**, following the footpath sign to The Nest. The path stays close to the right side of the field, and lovely views open up to the flat valley floor below. Cross three fields and three ladder stiles, and the field margin is now on the left, as is a small wood. At the end of this field, go through the gate into an old farmyard, and follow the driveway past the house (High Nest) and its garden with a fine show of snowdrops. The driveway leads out to the road, where we turn right along the A591 for just over 100m.and then turn left through a small wooden gate, on the path towards Walla Crag **(4).**

Walk on the edge of the field, with the fence to the right, and go through a gate and another field, to bend right to another gate and stile. Keep straight on and at the end of this field, turn right through a gate (or over the stile) and walk alongside a wall on the right, to another gate and stile. Keep straight ahead here along an old track, to a wooden kissing gate.

Turn left along the driveway and, after a few metres, notice a footpath going right. This leads along the stream and through a wood towards the edge of Keswick, for anyone needing a short cut to return quickly to the town.

The main route continues along the driveway, which soon divides, with the left fork only going to Rakefoot, and labelled Private, and our route is the right fork. At the end of the road, go right over the footbridge, then left, following the path, and begin to climb. A wall is on our right, and the stream is down to our left. Views to Skiddaw, Blencathra, and then down to the lakes on our right are magnificent during this ascent. Buzzards are often to be seen and heard.

Climb up and out on to the fells, with some grass and heather, and a long stone wall to our right. Near the top of the climb, is a kissing gate through the wall, and the views from the other side of the wall, are worth a detour. From here, the top of Walla Crag, are wonderful views including the near aerial view down into Derwent Water, with its little islands, and also a tiny delta where a river enters the lake. There is a much larger delta at the head (southern end) of the lake. It is possible to stay on the right side of the wall for a few hundred metres, and then return to our path.

Our walk continues on the left side of the wall, and as the path and wall begin to descend, we go left in a wide semicircular sweep on a nearly horizontal route, to avoid descending into the valley. A path does follow the wall and leads steeply to the road in the valley, and if a short cut is required, this would reduce the distance of the walk by a mile.

After swinging round the heads of the valley, we begin to descend and now the views are to the lake and up Borrowdale. Ashness Bridge will come into sight down below, and the narrow road leading up to Watendlath. Follow the path down for a long descent, with a very steep slope down to our right. At the bottom of this descent, pass through a gate and out on to the road **(5)**. Turn left briefly to visit the most photogenic and famous one arch pack horse bridge, but really we are turning right here to walk down the road.

The famous Ashness Bridge

Trees grow well in this sheltered valley, and line the road, as we descend to the valley floor. Pass a small parking space on the right and cross the cattle grid to reach the main Borrowdale road, the B 5289. Walk straight ahead along this road, with the lake on the left. After a few hundred metres, the lake shore and road part company, and our path is just off the road, walking through the woods where you may be fortunate enough to see a red squirrel. Reach Calfclose Bay, and at the far end of this bay, cross a footbridge over a small stream coming steeply down through Great Wood on Walla Crag. Bend left to follow the lake shore, heading west, as though out towards Rampsholme Island (National Trust) To the left of Rampsholme are the Scarf Stones, on which cormorants are often to be seen.

Gorse and broom grow along the shore, and gorse may be in flower even at this time of year. Look out for the huge split boulder of Borrowdale Volcanic rock **(6)**, with a sculpture to commemorate 1995, the Centenary Year of the National Trust. The architect was Peter Randall-Page and the rock shows an endless thread meandering 100 times through 10 annual rings and 10 segments to represent a centenary of growth.

Pass through a clump of conifers, on a drumlin, and then the path bends right to resume a northerly direction, and excellent views right show the steepness of Walla Crag. In the field to our right are small hills (Stable Hills) which are drumlins. Pass through a little wooden gate and off to the left is Lord's Island, another island under the care and management of the National Trust. The lake shore here has been fenced off, to protect the shore and enable lakeshore vegetation to grow.

The gravelled path bends right, away from the lake to pass a small group of houses, one of which is Stable Hills Cottage, a National Trust holiday cottage. Follow the drive away from the lake, but look out for a path to the left, at a large and small wooden gate. Take this path through The Ings, the delta of Brockle (Brockle = badger) Beck, a wooded wetland area with willow and alder, a great location for wild life. The gravelled path leads through to a gate and on into an open grassland area, with a small bay to our left, in which ducks, goosanders and even oyster catchers may be seen, and there are often herons to be seen on Lord's Island. Excavations on Lord's Island have found remains of a medieval settlement.

A seat with a view: from Friar's Crag along Derwent Water

Follow the path along the lakeside, passing Strandshag Bay, and go on through a wooden gate, then turn left up a few steps and out to a small headland **(7)**, which has been formed by a small volcanic intrusion of the hard rock dolerite. This is Friar's Crag and the site of the Ruskin Memorial, on which is written John Ruskin 1819-1900, together with his quote "The first thing which I remember as an event in life was being taken by my nurse to the brow of Friars Crag on Derwent Water". A large slab of local rock has been used for this memorial. Friars Crag is so called because Lindisfarne monks went from here to St Herbert's Island in the middle of the lake, to receive blessing from the hermit who lived there. The island is named after the hermit, Herbert, who was a disciple of St Cuthbert, Bishop of Lindisfarne in the 7th century. Two other literary connections with this location are that St Herbert's Island is the basis for the story of Beatrix Potter's Squirrel Nutkin sailing out to Owl Island, and Friar's Crag is thought to be the inspiration for the Darien Peak of Arthur Ransome.

Just continue along the lakeside path, with excellent views to Derwent Island and the big house just showing through the trees,

The Ruskin memorial on Friar's Crag

and reach another memorial, this time to Hardwicke Drummond Rawnsley (1851-1920). He was a Canon of Carlisle, Vicar of Crosthwaite (1883-1901) and one of the Founders of the National Trust. This stretch of Derwent Water's shore was given by subscribers who "desired that his name should not be forgotten" – (7th September 1922).

Walk on to reach a few houses, and then the road, passing Cockshot Wood on the right and at the lakeside are boats for hire, tea garden, toilets, and probably a few ducks and swans waiting to be fed. Pass the Lakeside car park and continue to the main road, across which is the town centre and the starting point of our walk.

February

Grasmere and Easedale

From the delightful busy village of Grasmere, the walk goes up the Easedale Valley and on to the fells, round the tarn, before descending back to the village. Then, in the opposite direction, walk past Dove Cottage and around Grasmere. Note the confusion of names, where the village and the lake are both referred to by the same word.

Length: 6 miles in Easedale valley and an extra 3½ miles round Grasmere. These two sections can be walked separately or together.

Time required: 3 hours or 4-5 hours

Terrain: includes a steep climb alongside Sour Milk Gill, followed by numerous marshy patches (unless the hills are covered by snow and ice). The walk round Grasmere is quite gentle, and on roads or good firm paths.

Map: 1:25,000 Outdoor Leisure map number 7, covering the South East of the English Lakes.

Starting point: Grasmere at one of the car parks, grid ref. 337074. The village is reached along the B5287, leading off the Windermere to Keswick road A591. Bus services link Grasmere with neighbouring towns.

Facilities: refreshments in many places in Grasmere, which also has a Tourist Information Centre (015394 35245).

Weather

This is the third and last official month of winter, and is often the coldest time of the year, though with more daylight than in January it is unlikely to be icy all month. Also the sun is beginning to give a little more warmth. Some Februarys can be very mild and 1998 was one of the warmest on record. Winter had gone, before it had really started. In Cumbria the daily maxima temperatures early in the month were about 6-7°C., and in mid month 10-11°C were common with 14°C recorded on a couple of days. Some of these mild days were dull and very wet, as most of the weather was coming from the Atlantic. *'February fill dyke'* was an appropriate expression. The only cool weather occurred in the first two days of the month, and the last few days, when a northerly spell brought colder weather, but only a slight dusting of snow. During this month the Scottish skiing

A stone boathouse along the shore of Grasmere

industry was severely hit by the lack of snow this year. The gloom and doom attitude suggests that we shall pay for this mild month, by cold weather over the next few weeks, but records show that a mild February is often followed by a mild March, though some years reveal a very cold month. An old saying that '*when it rains in February, the whole year suffers*', has undoubtedly applied to one or two years, but it has no real accuracy as a forecaster of the year ahead.

The countryside

Much of the countryside is looking brown at this time of year, with bracken, old leaves, stems and grasses dominating the colour, even where some green is beginning to show through. Hazel catkins are hanging and the first pussy willows are just showing, as signs of warmer days ahead. Many birds (starlings, rooks, lapwings) are still in winter flocks, but by the middle of the month, robins, thrushes and chaffinches will be singing and on sunny days the annual chasing begins as a prelude to pairing. Chaffinches are particularly active, but also blackbirds, blue tits and wood pigeons will be showing early signs of looking for mates. The earliest of breeders, notably the mistle thrushes, dippers and ravens will already be at their nests. On the lakes too, pairing is evident, with tufted duck, great crested grebe and goldeneye, but the last are mainly winter visitors although a few stay around throughout the summer too. Goosander are also mainly winter visitors, but a few of these birds do stay and breed. Buzzards may be seen and heard floating around overhead. The deciduous woodlands will still be wintry, though on the ground the earliest green shoots will be appearing, and in a mild year (e.g. 1998) hawthorn hedges show a little green before the end of the month. In the larch plantations, sprouts of green as well tiny pink flowers will be evident by the end of the month – and in areas of coniferous trees do keep a look out for red squirrels. In gardens and on roadsides snowdrops are abundant and the first yellow is showing through on the daffodils. Early flowering azaleas were in colour by the end of the month this year. A few gardens in Grasmere not only had their snowdrops and daffodils out, but the grass had received its first cutting of the year by the 28th – the sign of a very mild winter.

Grasmere

The reputation of the past has been maintained to the present day. Wordsworth described the village as 'the loveliest spot that man hath ever found', and Thomas Gray called it 'this little unsuspected paradise'. They must both have been thinking of bright and sunny days! This popular tourist village is busy throughout the year, and has hotels, bed and breakfast establishments and many shops catering for tourists, including the Heaton Cooper Studio, and the famed Sarah Nelson Gingerbread Shop where gingerbread has been made since 1850. Sarah is buried in the churchyard, and her secret recipe is still being used. The Gingerbread Shop is next door to the church, not one of Grasmere's most attractive buildings from the outside, but containing a wealth of interest both inside and in the churchyard.

St Oswald's Church is dedicated to St Oswald, King of Northumbria in the 7th century, and part of the present church dates from the 13th century. The interior is noted for the exposed wooden beams in the roof, and the low arches between the nave and the north aisle. The original nave wall is now in the middle of the church, serving as a support for the roof, ever since the north aisle was built as an extension in the 17th century. At that time the north wall was not pulled down, but merely pierced at intervals. The medieval tower has walls 3-4 feet thick, made of stones taken from the stream. Wordsworth's Prayer Book is displayed in the showcase be-

Goldeneye on Grasmere

Dora's gravestone in Grasmere churchyard

Inside the gravestone illustration:

> DORA QUILLINAN,
> 9ᵀᴴ DAY OF JULY
> 1847
> Him that cometh to me
> I will in no wise cast out
> ST JOHN 6ᵀᴴ Chap. 37ᵀᴴ Ver.

hind the choir stalls, and in the churchyard, eight of the yew trees were planted by Wordsworth in 1819. William Wordsworth (1850) and his wife Mary (1859) are buried near the yew trees, and in the next grave is their daughter Dora, who married Edward Quillinan. Wordsworth's sister Dorothy is buried in the grave next to Dora. Just along the road from the church is the site for the Grasmere Sports, held annually in August, every year since 1852.

Dove Cottage

The home of William Wordsworth and his sister Dorothy, from 1799-1808, this tiny cottage contains memorabilia of their lives here, including Dorothy's Journal of their daily life. In 1802, after his marriage to Mary, Wordsworth brought her to live here as well. The cottage is open daily for guided tours from mid February, and there is a delightful garden extending up the hillside from the back of the cottage. There is a gift shop and a tea shop, and the Wordsworth Museum is nearby. This award winning museum contains more memorabilia and various manuscripts, portraits as well as paintings. Rydal Mount, where Wordsworth lived from 1813-1850, is about two miles away, just off the road to Ambleside. Thomas De Quincy, who first visited Wordsworth at Dove Cottage in 1807, came and lived in the cottage from 1809-1835. During the last 25 years, the garden at Dove Cottage has been restored by the custodian to what it was like during Wordsworth's lifetime. Information in letters and journals enabled him to discover what used to be growing here, and seeds and plants have been brought in, even though many are not growing in the Lake District nowadays. For example, in Wordsworth's time many fields grew corn and their associated flowers, but now there are no arable fields within miles of Dove Cottage.

White Moss Common

This low-lying area is located between Grasmere and Rydal Water, and part of it is a wetland, noted for its plants and bird life. It is a popular area with visitors, and has parking spaces on both sides of the main road. Footpaths lead from here in all directions.

The Walk

Leave the car park, (whichever one you have chosen) and from the centre of the village **(1)**, take the Easedale Road, signposted to Easedale Tarn. Walk along this narrow road for nearly 800m and pass the turning to the Youth Hostel at Thorny How. Just beyond Easedale Cottage, where the road bends to the right, go left following the sign to Easedale Tarn, whereas straight on along the road is signposted Far Easedale, Borrowale and Helm Crag **(2)**. Go over a slab footbridge, through a few trees and out into the valley, then pass through a gate and walk along the broad stony path.

Soon reach, but ignore, a modern stone bridge (1997) crossing the stream to our right, as we keep straight on along a very clear path. The stream is well banked here, in order to reduce flooding, which is always likely after heavy rain as the Lake District rocks are impervious and so run off is rapid. Floods occur quickly, but subside quickly too.

Much of the path has been lined with stones, both to reduce human erosion and also to reduce muddiness, but often making the path uneven, so watch where you are putting your feet. Well-soled boots are vital. Just keep walking ahead, with the views of the waterfall indicating our route, and after passing through the wooden kissing gate, begin to climb. The path stays close to the foaming waterfall of Sourmilk Gill, and in the shelter of the valley notice how a few holly and juniper survive in a very damp environment.

As the path levels off at the top of the fall **(3)**, we begin to bend round to the left. A few metres down to the right near the stream are several juniper trees, and just beyond these are small mounds,

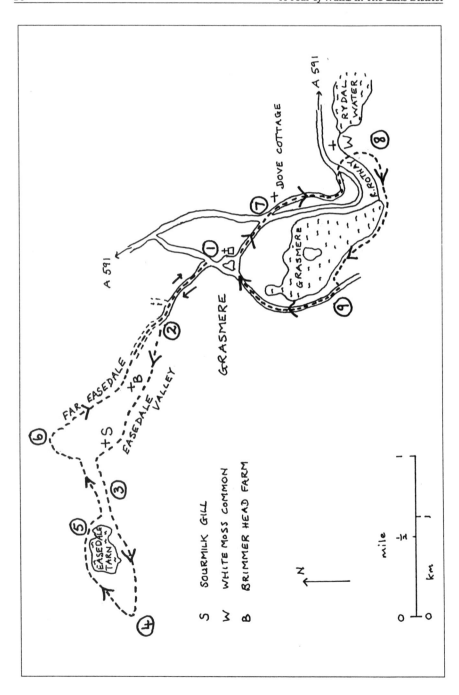

The footpath near Sourmilk Gill

which are of morainic debris left by a glacier. These are the oldest, smallest and furthest downstream of the morainic mounds to be seen on this walk.

As the path begins to climb again, a small wood of juniper can be seen away to the left. Keep climbing until the tarn comes into view, in its magnificent basin, surrounded by hills. The poet de Quincy thought the tarn and its surrounding mountains to be very impressive and described Easedale Tarn as 'the most gloomily sublime' of the Lake District tarns. On the left of the path, near where the stream leaves the tarn, are the remnants of the former refreshment hut which served walkers in Victorian times. Continue along the path to the left of the lake, and here, as earlier in the walk there are likely to be very wet patches to cross, often made easier by carefully laid stepping stones.

The fairly level stretch goes along to the far end of the lake, where a small delta can be seen, formed by deposits from the stream. Beyond the delta is a lone tree, which we will be passing shortly. First we pass a lone tree near our path, and on our left are several uneven

but quite steep mounds – morainic debris pushed and dumped by a
glacier. As our path draws closer to this stream, notice the water descending steeply from the slope ahead. We are not going up there, although if the weather is good and anyone wishes to do so, the steep
climb will reveal Codale Tarn, a small lake at a higher level.

As these mounds of debris end, notice the steep black rocks of Eagle Crag to our left (4). This was a corrie back wall, and at its foot is a
flat and marshy area, formerly a small lake in a hollow carved out by
ice, but filled in with vegetation during the last few thousand years.

Look for a suitable crossing point to turn right across the stream to
begin our return journey, towards the lone tree (a juniper) seen earlier. Once across the stream walk through the bracken, along a thin
grassy path which crosses several wet patches, and leads round to
the other side of the lake, near an old sheep fold. The path becomes
clearer as we walk along the side of the lake. It then has to cross several small but steep undulations which are the mounds of terminal
morainic debris left by an advance of a glacier thousands of years
ago – and contributing to the damming and hence formation of the
lake. In the midst of these mounds are a few hollows which can be
quite marshy (5), and these are known as kettle holes, probably the
location of huge ice boulders left in the moraine as the ice was melting.

The path leads round to the river's outlet from the lake, and here
we do not cross over but turn left to begin our descent, with
Sourmilk Gill on our right. Follow the path on the left side of the valley, and where the stream bends right to go over the waterfalls (3),
we keep straight ahead and begin to descend towards Far Easedale.
As our path bends left, on the far side of the valley can be seen a
walled area with trees inside it. It is 30 years since the wall was re-
paired to keep sheep out, in order to see how successful the tree
growth would be in the protected area.

The path bends left, and then curves round to the right as it descends to Far Easedale Gill. Cross over the footbridge and turn right
to follow the track downstream (6), with the tumbling stream on our
right. Where this stream bends right away from our path, look out for
some huge ice smoothed boulders on the left. The path is very rocky.
Pass an old barn on the left and a few conifers including an araucaria
pine (monkey puzzle). To the right is Brimmer Head Farm, and a
small wood is on the left.

Our track is now between stone walls and is joined by the route from Helm Crag coming in from our left. Turn right through an iron gate, on to a stony and partially paved driveway. On our left is a permissive path through Lancrigg Woods but we keep straight on, to pass Easedale House and reach a narrow surfaced road. Follow this across an open grassy patch, with Helm Crag clearly seen up to the left. Pass the entrance to Lancrigg Vegetarian Country House Hotel, and reach the bridge where we started our walk up the valley (2), and just keep going along the road to return to Grasmere. Lancrigg House was where Wordsworth wrote most of "The Prelude".

Extension walk round the lake

Walk from the village passing the church, the car park and the open field on the left. At the main road cross straight over to the minor road (7) signposted to Dove Cottage. A guided tour of the small cottage and a visit to the museum are highly recommended.

For the walk round the lake, walk along the narrow road, which was formerly the main road, and soon begin to climb, between stone walls and cottages. Climb up to How Top, where a path and narrow road go left, but we keep straight ahead, and good views over Grasmere now open up. Follow the road as it undulates and winds, to reach a small car park on the right with seats to the left. Good views to Rydal Water can be seen ahead, as we descend quite steeply to the main road near a car park in the old quarry.

Walk into the car park and look at the Information Board, with its map of this area – which is White Moss Common. Cross over the road, – which can be quite hazardous. Go down a few steps and follow the path to the footbridge. Cross over the river and here there is a choice of paths. We could turn left into the Wetland conservation area, or go right along the river bank, but our route is straight ahead, to climb into the woods, following the signpost to the viewpoint on Loughrigg Terrace. The woods are carpeted with cuckoo pint and colourful flowers in the spring, and are very rich in bird life. Various tits and finches as well as greater spotted woodpeckers are likely to be seen or heard in any month, and a dipper may be noticed along the river.

At the top edge of woods go through a wooden gate between stone slabs, to merge on to a well worn path. Turn right to climb up to a viewpoint **(8)** and a junction of four paths. We turn right to descend towards the River Rothay and the outlet from Grasmere, and our route is straight ahead on the stony beach along the left side of the lake. Go through a wooden kissing gate, passing the notice saying the fishing is private (for W.A.D.A.A. members). The path rises a few metres away from the lake but keeps straight ahead through a few trees, and views across to the village of Grasmere open up – with hills and beautiful views all around – possibly enhanced by snow at this time of the year. Keen bird watchers may spot some interesting birds on the lake, including coots, various ducks (mallard, tufted, goldeneye), Canada geese, swans, great crested grebes and herring gulls, which may be harassing grebes for any fish that they have caught. Herons, which may already be nesting, are often to be seen on the island in the middle of the lake.

Walk on through a gate and follow the well-worn path alongside the lake, and then a grassy field to the left, and a stone boathouse on the lakeside (merging with the landscape), and a large house up to the left. Pass a lakeside seat, go through a wooden gate, pass another seat, and keep going. Just before another boathouse, turn left to leave the lake, and walk between wire fences, with a lovely stone house to the right of the path. Climb up a ladder stile to reach the narrow road **(9)**, and turn right.

Pass a wetland area on the right, at the end of the lake (as is true of the ends of many of the lakes), and begin to pass one or two houses. On the left is the large garden of Silver Howe, with prolific growth of rhododendrons and possibly early flowering azaleas. Reach Pavement End cottage, which, although there is no pavement, is the edge of the village, and we soon reach the T.I.C., the church, and our starting point.

March

Gowbarrow and Aira Force

This rather short walk passes through the sheltered Aira Valley and returns across the exposed fells, through what seems like a different world and certainly experiences a different climate.

Length: 6 miles, though it is possible to walk up one side of the valley to Dockray and then return on the other side of the valley without going over Gowbarrow Fell.

Time required: 3-4 hours.

Terrain: begins as a made path but becomes a steep and sometimes rocky climb past the waterfalls, and part of the walk over the fell is likely to be wet underfoot. Scenery in the valley is magnificent with some wonderful views looking out over Ullswater.

Map: 1:25,000 O.S. Outdoor Leisure map 5, The English Lakes North Eastern area.

Starting point: grid ref. 402201. The National Trust car park at Aira Force is on the A592 from Windermere to Penrith, which are the two nearest towns. There are railway stations at both of these towns and a bus service runs along this road.

Facilities: a tea shop is adjacent to the car park and a choice of refreshment is available in Glenridding at the southern end of the lake. Both nearby towns have Tourist Information Centres (Windermere phone is 015394 46499, and Penrith 01768 867466).

Weather

A month which often brings heavy rain or heavy snowfalls, interspersed with dry, fresh or bracing weather, when the wind blows from the north, March was more noted for mild weather and heavy rain this year. There were many wet days when rainfall in the valleys exceeded half an inch (12mm). Daily maxima temperatures were 5-6°C early in the month, but generally 10° or more for the last three weeks of the month. This was the fifth consecutive month above average. The old saying *'As it rains in March, So it rains in June'*, enables the pessimists to predict a wet June, but fortunately there is no direct connection between these two months. The driest weather came in mid month when high pressure dominated the weather for nearly two weeks, and the 20th-22nd were particularly sunny. By the end of the month the days are lengthening and British Summer Time has begun, so optimism is increasing, as birds begin to sing and plants begin to grow. The sun still has little warmth though it reaches the equator on its northward travels.

William Morris wrote of March:

slayer of the winter, art thou here again?
O welcome, thou that bringst the Summer nigh!

The countryside

More famous than William Morris as a poet, is William Wordsworth, and his daffodils are perhaps the most famous flowers to occur in poetry. It is believed that he was thinking of Gowbarrow when he wrote some of his most famous lines. There are still many hosts to be seen, and in 1998 they were in flower earlier than would have been normal in Wordsworth's time. Many other flowers were out early, including violets, primroses and celandines. Grass was also growing and availability of pasture helped to reduce the need for as much feed for farm animals. Sheep and a few cattle could be seen in the valleys and on the fells. The first buds appeared on some of the trees and in the woods the woodpeckers were becoming noisy. Green woodpeckers were calling their yaffling laughter, and the greater spotted were drumming violently on the trees. It is only because of their unique head structure they are able to hammer hard and fast on the tree trunks, without knocking themselves out, as would happen to other birds or animals if they tried. The greater spotted wood-

Fellside scene in March

pecker is a very handsome bird with its bold black and white marking, and the bright red patch on the lower belly. The male also has a red patch on the nape. On the rivers, dippers will be controlling their territory ready for the breeding season which generally begins by the end of this month. They often nest behind waterfalls, where they are safe from predators. These remarkable birds not only fly through waterfalls, but walk into streams, searching for their food amongst the rocks on the stream bed. They can cope even in fast flowing streams, but have become less numerous in many of their traditional haunts possibly because of water pollution. On the hills, the pipits are moving back to their breeding areas and the ravens will be sitting on eggs. Ducks and waders are still around, although they begin to migrate north for breeding. Meanwhile, a few of the earliest wheatears and perhaps ring ouzels will be arriving from the south. A few of the trees in the sheltered valleys have catkins or blossom, and the early greenery is showing by the end of the month.

William Wordsworth

It is believed that the legend of the knight Sir Eglamore may have

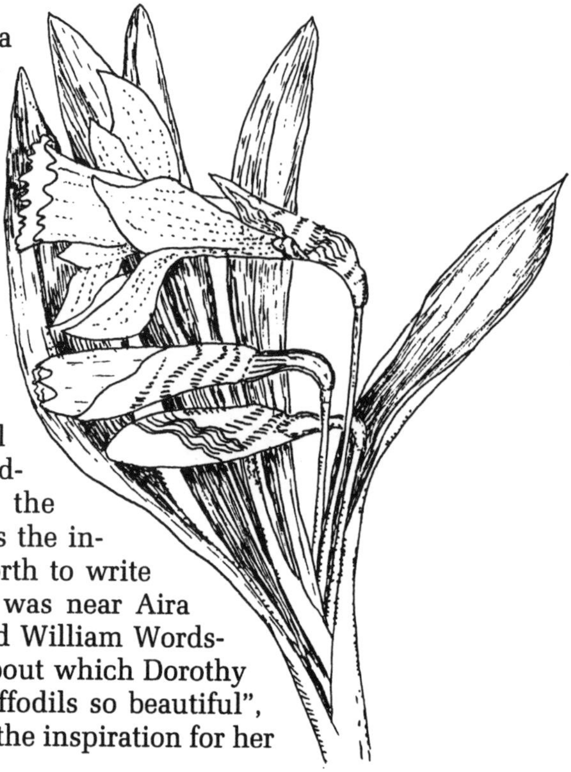

been set near Aira
Force. Whilst the
knight was away at
the crusades, Emma
of Greystoke, his be-
trothed often went
sleepwalking in this
valley, but on his re-
turn in the middle of
the night, he saw her
near Aira Force and
his delight at seeing
her caused him to call
out, and she woke sud-
denly and fell on to the
rocks. This legend was the inspiration for Wordsworth to write
The Somnambulist. It was near Aira
Force that Dorothy and William Wordsworth saw daffodils about which Dorothy
wrote "I never saw daffodils so beautiful",
and this was probably the inspiration for her
brother to write:

> *I wandered lonely as a cloud*
> *That floats on high o'er vales and hills*
> *When all at once I saw a crowd*
> *A host of golden daffodils.*
> *Beside the lake, beneath the trees*
> *Fluttering and dancing in the breeze.*

Imagine yourself writing these words on the shores of Ullswater or
in the woods near Aira Force.

Hanging valleys

When ice was carving deep valleys such as that containing the 7
mile long Ullswater, the rivers flowing from the adjacent hills were
unable to erode as quickly as the glacier. When the climate warmed
up and the ice had all melted, the tributaries were left at a much
higher level, and formed what are now called hanging valleys. In or-

der to descend from these higher valleys down to the main U-shaped valley they have to drop very quickly; picturesque steep, fast and tumbling streams are formed, and they may even have waterfalls and cascades as can be seen along Aira Beck.

Aira Force

The main fall has a height of 65ft (20m) and occurs in the hanging valley where the beck is flowing at the meeting place of the Skiddaw slates and the Borrowdale volcanics. The main waterfall, as well as the smaller falls, drops over outcrops of hard rock. High Force is further upstream and is smaller but has cut a deep chasm. The local names, force and beck are of Norse origin, meaning waterfall and stream respectively, and aira means a gravel bank.

Gowbarrow Park

The fell land in the Park was formerly a medieval deer park, and the lower slopes down to the lake were managed as woodland where coppicing took place, and charcoal and tannin were also produced. The Howard family landscaped the valley near the Force, planted half a million trees, and created footpaths and built bridges. In 1846, below the force, they began to create an arboretum, which can be seen on this walk. More than 200 firs and pines collected from all over the world were brought here, including the giant sitka spruce. The valley became a popular location for visitors more than a hundred years ago, and has retained that popularity, being more popular than ever nowadays.

Lyulph's Tower

Castellated Lyulph's Tower was the hunting lodge in Gowbarrow Park. The present building dates from 1782 and was built for the Earl of Surrey, who later became the Duke of Norfolk. Previous lodges had been on the same site, originally for the Howards of Greystoke. The opening line from "The Somnambulist" is:

List ye who pass by Lyulph's tower

The Walk

Start from the National Trust car park **(1)** at Aira Force alongside
Ullswater. Walk out at the end of the car park and along a broad gravelled path through a wooded area with the trees just beginning to
show their green. Go through a gate and across a small stream (not
the main stream) and bend left, where straight ahead can be seen a
bridge over the main stream, which is the direction of our return
walk. As we bend to the left and continue upstream, the patch of

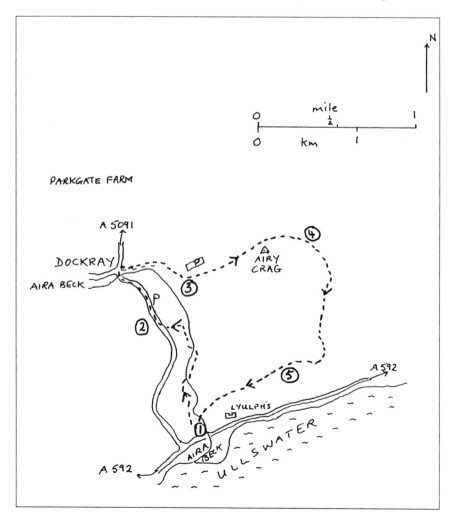

grassland on the right is coloured by daffodils. We move on through a variety of conifers, in the old Victorian Arboretum, which includes a fine araucaria pine, the monkey-puzzle tree. The main beck is now down to our right, as the path climbs slightly. Note the brown staining in the water from the iron leached from the rocks.

The first leaves of many wild flowers will be showing, although many will be more colourful in April, May or even June. Wood sorrel with its heart-shaped leaves and white flowers can be seen, as well as violets, and large numbers of primroses.

The path is stepped in places and a parallel path on the other side of the stream may be noticed. Pass through an area of rhododendrons, and as we climb the view left over Ullswater opens out, and then the main waterfall comes into sight. Aira Force can look truly magnificent if the recent weather has been wet (which it often has been in the Lake District). Pass the steps leading down to the bottom of the waterfall, and follow the path as it goes to the memorial stone bridge at the top of the falls.

Cross over the bridge and turn left, upstream, now on the right bank. Notice in the stream the huge boulders which have been moved by the water when in spate, and smoothed by the water for many thousands of years. It is amazing just how much power the rushing water must have. Walk on up this beautiful valley as far as a wooden bridge, then cross over, back to the other side of the stream, and continue upstream, passing the deep and narrow chasms cut by the water. This is High Force and above here is the turbulent stretch of river known as the Cascades.

Dippers live in this area and may be seen bobbing and curtseying on rocks, before they

Aira Force

walk into the stream in their quest for food. Tree creepers and nuthatches are also resident through the year – as are red squirrels. By the end of April or early May, these woods will have the sounds of many warblers, as well as pied flycatchers when all the summer migrants arrive. This sheltered river valley is a wonderful nature reserve for birds and flowers.

Dipper on Aira Beck

Where the path goes right, using large rocks as stepping stones to reach the other side of the stream, we go left through a small gate in the wall, and cross the field to a kissing gate and a car park in an old quarry. Turn right along the road **(2)**, and if you look back at the valley, it is so deeply incised as to be almost invisible. Across the valley on the opposite slope can be seen a small wood of conifers, alongside which our path continues later.

Walk along the road, passing Parkgate Farm, with daffodils along its drive, and then we walk down into Dockray. The gentle stream on the right has to descend to the level of Ullswater, a much deeper valley cut by a glacier, and this has led to the formation of the waterfalls we have walked past. Cross over the river bridge, with the Royal Hotel on the left, offering coffee, bar meals and accommodation if required. The road bends right and then left but, just before the left bend, go right along a stony track following the footpath sign to Aira Force and Ulcat Row, and then pass through a farm. The track descends slightly, through a gate and then passes Millses and you may notice the curlew wind vane on the barn to the right of the path. Cross a wooden footbridge over Ridings Beck, where marsh marigolds grow in the stream, and when the track splits, keep straight on signposted to Gowbarrow and Aira Force. Some of the gorse will be in flower, and stonechats may be seen around here. Once through the gate into the next field, turn immediately left **(3)** to follow the permissive footpath to Gowbarrow.

Climb up the field with the wall on the left, and over the stile at the top of the field, and keep climbing, with the coniferous wood on the left. The steep ascent brings us up to the height where bilberry and heather grow, and then the path begins to level off. The triangulation point at the highest point of Gowbarrow Fell is at Airy Crag 1578ft (481m), and a small detour can be made here if desired, though the path keeps on close to the wall, and then begins to descend.

Just before reaching the wall at the end of this section of the fell, where a ladder stile goes left, we turn right **(4)** to follow a small valley and our path is on the right side of the stream, parallel to the wall beyond the stream, Collierhagg Beck. This narrow path passes through bracken and reaches an old ruined shooting lodge near where there is an A stile going left towards the woods. We turn right, and just follow the path.

The path soon rises above a large steep rocky outcrop called Yew Crag – an outcrop of Borrowdale volcanic rocks. We cross a gully containing a stream and then another gully with a wooden bridge. Wonderful views of Ullswater open up, with the massive fells beyond. Numerous clumps of primroses grow on the slopes which we are now crossing. The path skirts along the hillside and when the path splits, the right fork climbs slightly but we go left and slightly down, to reach a stone memorial seat **(5)**. Wheatears may be seen around here later in the year.

Last year's bracken covers much of the hillside, though a few windswept trees survive here too. As our path descends steeply, a large house down to the left becomes much clearer – and the turreted towers can be seen. This is Lyulph's Tower.

We are joined by a fairly level path coming from the left, and once past the large house the path divides, with the right fork climbing slightly, but we take the left fork which is really straight on, to reach a wooden stile over a wire fence. We soon begin to descend to the valley and the path is stepped in places. On our descent into the valley notice how the climate and vegetation are different from the open fell – it is like entering a different world. Pass some huge fir trees on the right and a few cherries on the left, possibly with blossom. The noise of water takes over from the noise of the wind which is likely to have dominated out on the open hillside, which is appropriately named Gowbarrow, the word meaning windy hill. The stepped path descends to the wooden footbridge over the main stream. Walk on to the open grassy area seen earlier, and follow the main path through the gate and back to the car park, where very brave or tame chaffinches may be waiting to help eat up any remaining food. Jackdaws are also prominent in the car park area and rooks will be nesting in a few of the taller trees.

April

Langdale

The walk includes a gentle stretch along the valley floor through farmland and woods, and a steep climb to Harrison Stickle, giving some of the best views in the Lake District. These two parts can be taken separately for a half day, or linked together for a good day's walking. In bad weather with poor visibility the higher section should only be attempted by fit walkers, with adequate clothing, food and drink and a compass, as well as the local map.

Length: 5½ miles in the valley, plus 3 more for the climb up to Harrison. Time required: allow 3 hours and another 2 hours.

Terrain: undulating at low level but then very steep and rocky in places, for the extension section.

Map: O.S. 1:25,000 Outdoor Leisure map number 6, South Western area of the English Lakes.

Starting point: car park at the New Dungeon Ghyll, GR295065. This is reached along the B5343 from Ambleside. Occasional buses run from Ambleside.

Facilities: available at the starting point and at other pubs along the valley. Nearest T.I.C. is at Ambleside (015394 32582).

Weather

Numerous annual visits to Langdale at this time of year have revealed Stickle Tarn bathed in sunshine, or icebound with the surrounding hills covered in snow – clothing requirements varying from shirt sleeves to balaclavas. 1998 served to emphasise the variety of weather which can be experienced. There were a few of the *'sweet April showers, which do bring May flowers'*, as quoted in "Five

Pied flycatcher

Hundred points of Good Husbandry", but there were also days of heavy and prolonged rain which produced the wettest April since 1818. Maximum daily temperatures were generally about 8-10°C, which meant that the grass was just beginning to grow, and a few days of warm weather saw temperatures rise to a very mild 15°C on the 24th and 25th. Sunny days occurred in the 2nd and 4th weeks, with very wet days in between. Around Easter there was a cold spell and several centimetres of snow fell, though there was less snow than in Scotland and north Wales, and fewer floods than in parts of the Midlands. The cold spell seemed even worse than it might have done, because the previous weeks and months of winter had been so mild. The land was wet and waterlogged, and tumbling streams and waterfalls were at their most impressive, adding to the beauties of the landscape.

The countryside

Oh to be in England,
now that April's there
And whoever wakes in England
Sees some morning, unaware
That the lowest boughs and the brushwood sheaf
Round the elm tree bole are in tiny leaf,
While the chaffinch sings on the orchard bough,
In England – now.

Robert Browning wrote lovingly of England in "Home thoughts, from Abroad" and captured some of the features of April. The trees are always beginning to show their green leaves during this month, though elm trees are not as numerous as in Browning's time. Chaf-

Looking down Great Langdale Valley

finches as well as many other small birds are singing lustily, as they establish their territory or try to attract a mate, by their impressive performances.

The resident birds such as robin and blackbird are singing too, and by the end of the month are joined in the valleys by the early chiffchaffs and some willow warblers, with wheatears appearing on the hillsides. Crows, ravens, buzzards and pipits may also be seen on the fells. Gulls are around all year, though many which were merely winter visitors will have departed by the end of the month.

The valley is very green with pasture growing and the hillsides beginning to lose their dull brownish winter coloration. The landscape of Great Langdale has been strongly influenced by glaciation, with the steep sided but flat floored valley being a typical result of ice erosion. The valley sides have many small streams flowing swiftly down them, most notable being Mill Gill (popularly known as Stickle Ghyll, as named on the O.S. map), and these are called hanging valleys. The valley floor is very flat in places, where former lakes created in hollows gouged out by ice erosion and then filled with meltwater, have been filled in by sedimentation causing deltas which have filled up the entire lakes. In between the former lakes are rocky areas never eroded by the ice, and these now create waterfalls as at Skelwith Bridge. The hillsides have been scraped smooth by ice, but several locations protruded above the ice and these were affected by freezing and thawing which creates rough and jagged features. These are called *nunataks*, an Eskimo word, as these features can be seen in northern Canada today, and also in Antarctica where they protrude through the ice cover as black lumps. Outstanding examples of nunataks in the Langdale valley are the top of Pavey Ark, the Pike of Stickle and Harrison Stickle. Several local names are of Norse origin, for example Langdale meaning long valley and pike meaning a pointed hill.

Quarrying

Several small and disused quarries will be seen on this walk, and the largest is walked through near Elterwater. Formerly a large employer, quarrying has almost ceased, but much of the local stone is evident in the buildings as well as the miles of stone walls. A major use for the rock now is in tourist souvenirs, as can be seen in the showrooms at Skelwith Bridge and in many shops in the towns.

In Elterwater Quarry

Many of the quarries are clothed with trees and often used as car parks, as at White Moss Common (February walk) and in Borrowdale (November walk).

The Farming Year

In the Langdale Valley the traditional farming type was rearing sheep, and a very skilful, though no longer profitable, use of the harsh landscape had evolved. The sheep would winter on the fells, though may be brought down in severe weather and often be supplied with extra feed. Lambing would take place in April and May, down in the inbye – the fields near the farm. The sheep and lambs would soon move to the intake fields on the lower slopes and then up on to the fells. Shearing and dipping would be in late summer, followed by the sale of the lambs. The fields in the valleys would be used for hay making throughout the summer.

Chapel Stile

This tiny village set into the bottom of the valley side, shares its church and school with Elterwater, only a mile to the east. There were quarries in the valley though there are now houses in the quarry, and the large quarry on the hillside to the south of the village is still working though on a much smaller scale than formerly, producing the attractive green slate. (In strict geological terms it is not really slate but a volcanic rock which can be split into slate-shaped pieces, as well as being cut into larger slabs for decorative building work). Holy Trinity church was built in 1856 and merges with the rocks on the valley wall behind it.

The Walk

The valley walk is a gentle though undulating walk beginning from the large National Trust car park at the New Dungeon Ghyll Hotel **(1)**. Go out to the road and turn left for a few metres and then right through a gate, along a stony track over the river. Follow the track which bends right and then left to the gate into the farmyard, and then leave the farmyard through a gate to the left. Pass over a small footbridge and follow the clear path alongside a small stream through one field to a kissing gate. Then the path begins to rise diag-

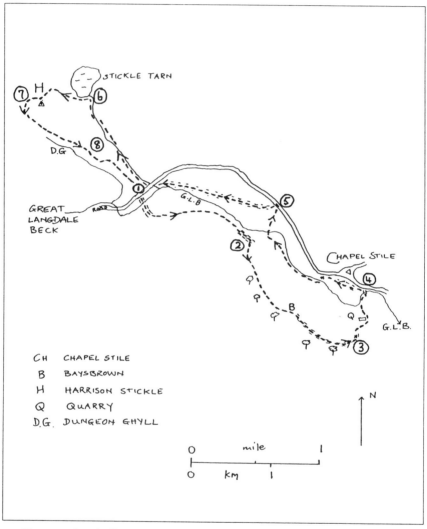

CH   CHAPEL STILE
B   BAYSBROWN
H   HARRISON STICKLE
Q   QUARRY
D.G. DUNGEON GHYLL

onally up the hillside through grass and bracken, on the lower slopes of Lingmoor Fell. There are a few trees on the valley floor nearby and on the lower sides of the valley, and though mainly deciduous, there are a few conifers and a small entirely coniferous plantation. A few junipers grow on the slopes up to the right. The main river, the Great Langdale beck is down to the left, and is mostly embanked to control flow and reduce flooding.

A few bluebells grow alongside this path, and their leaves should be showing by the beginning of April, and pipits will be calling and singing around here. Go on through a kissing gate, and a clear undulating path progresses along the hillside, with places where the path has been made of stones, to reduce wear and tear. We reach a section of path between stone walls, and then pass an isolated farm and barn, Oak Howe, where the path turns right (2). It soon bends left and climbs slightly. All around are likely to be sheep, with lambs appearing by the end of the month.

Go on through another gate, beyond which is a huge slab of rock, smoothed by ice originally and then by water for the past few thousand years. There is a very flat valley floor down to the left, and this was formerly a lake which filled a hollow eroded by ice during the Ice Age. Since that time, rivers carrying sediment gradually filled up the lake, to create a very flat landscape, accentuated by the steep sides of the valley.

Walk into a small wood, with a few larch at first, showing a little greenery, and then some broadleaved deciduous. Up to the right can be seen evidence of former quarrying. Pass to the right of Baysbrown (name originating from Bruni's cowshed) Farm where swallows may be seen by the end of the month, and keep straight ahead along the surfaced driveway. Hummocks of glacial debris and a few hard rock remnants can be seen in the fields down to the left. We then enter Baysbrown Wood where green and greater spotted woodpeckers and goldcrests are amongst the birds to be seen or heard, as well as early summer visitors, chiffchaff and willow warbler. The large expanses of bluebells will be growing up and the early signs of wood sorrel with its distinctively shaped leaves grows alongside the road, and many of the trees including larch will be sprouting greenery.

Reach a house on the left where we turn left (3) off the surfaced drive on to a stony track through a metal gate, with wild garlic in the woods to the left, and cherry blossom on trees to the right. Walk into and through the old quarry workings – and beware, there may be an explosion in the working part of the quarry. Bend right into the quarry and once past the large black sheds, go left along the drive out of the quarry. After a few metres go left off this track on to a stony path leading downhill to the left of a house. This leads to the river where we turn right, downstream, as far as the footbridge over the Great Langdale Beck. Cross over and turn left along the road, passing (or visiting) the Wainwright Inn **(4)**, and a few metres further along the road turn left following the footpath sign, to pass behind the village school, unless you wish to call in at the village shop which is along the road. The path reaches a tarmac lane where we turn left, and when the track splits take the right fork passing Throng Farm and then along the path to the right of the buildings, through a small gate and on the path between two stone walls.

Reach a stony track and turn left. The road is a few metres up to the right, for anyone who has followed the road through the village. Notice the modern houses alongside this road, built on the site of a former quarry. Follow the track to the stone bridge, built 1818, and once across the river turn right.

Walk alongside the river, with good views ahead and up to the left, which is where we were walking an hour or so ago, up near Baysbrown Farm. The valley floor can now be seen as a very flat surface – a former lake bed. The first field we pass through is used for camping, which is very popular in the Lake District, though controlled and regulated by the National Park Authority. We follow the river side through four fields, on this easy return journey, and when Oak Howe is up to our left, turn right over a footbridge, gated at both ends, to control sheep rather than walkers. A bridge was built here in memory of R.W. "Bill" Bailey (1912-1980), "Who loved to walk in the Lake District", and was rebuilt in 1983, by the Upland Management Service, financed by the Friends of the Lake District. With well over 6000 members this important group actively campaigns to protect the natural beauty of the Lake District.

Cross the meadows, where pipits may be singing and by the end of the month the first lambs can be seen, and at the road turn left **(5)**. After 100m turn left along a stony track signposted public byway footpath to Dungeon Ghyll, with a post box in the wall where we turn. This track leads on for a mile back to our starting point. Just before reaching the end of this walk, look out for some green caravans (painted as camouflage) over to the right on the lower valley side. Notice also, the woods on a few of the lower slopes and the green fields, which are smaller than the large browner areas of the intake higher on the hillside.

Reach our starting point in the National Trust car park which is well screened by trees, both deciduous and larch, which are just coming into leaf, and frequented by jackdaws, robins and chaffinches, eager to help eat up your sandwiches.

Extension

If you have time and are feeling energetic, a walk up to Harrison Stickle, one of the Langdale Pikes will take nearly two hours – but is well worth the time and effort. Unless you are an experienced walker, the ascent to the Pike is not advisable in poor weather, and it is essential to take food, drink, warm and waterproof clothing, and a map and compass.

The climb to the Pike should be taken slowly, and can be divided into three parts, going up to Stickle Tarn first, then continuing on to the pike, and descending down the steep valley of Dungeon Ghyll.

Start from the car park **(1)** adjacent to the Sticklebarn Tavern (open all day and all year, and also offering Bunkhouse accommodation) and the New Dungeon Ghyll Hotel. Go through to the rear of the buildings and the path soon divides – straight on is our path, the route to Stickle Tarn, and the left fork is the line of our return from the steep descent of Dungeon Ghyll.

A clear and stony path goes up alongside Mill Gill, and climbs steeply to Stickle Tarn, a magnificent corrie lake with the dramatic back wall of Pavey Ark. A dam **(6)** holds up the water of the lake, and it was originally constructed to help regulate the water flow down to the valley, and to supply the former gunpowder factory at Elterwater.

Turn left along the dam and follow the path climbing steeply up the scree slopes; ascend to a low gap between Harrison Stickle on the left and Pavey Ark over to the right. The path passes two small tarns and then turns left for a short climb up the rocks to the top of Harrison. This should reveal magnificent views down the full length of the Langdale valley, over Elterwater where the old slate quarry can be seen, to Windermere in the distance. There is also the view across the valley into Little Langdale and a ring of peaks in all directions.

From Harrison Stickle go down and to the left, heading westwards and descending into the valley **(7)** between Harrison and Pike of Stickle. Turn left before reaching the stream, and skirt along the bottom of Harrison Stickle, passing through a rocky area where a little scrambling may be necessary. The scree slope here is thought to be the site of a prehistoric stone axe factory. An alternative is to go across the small stream (Dungeon Ghyll), and down the other side of its valley, passing between the two rocky areas of Thorn Crag and

Loft Crag, which leads to a clear path down the far side of Dungeon Ghyll.

However if going down the near side of the valley, with the stream to our right, once beyond the rocks a clear stony path crosses a grassy area, and is marked with small cairns. This is not yet very steep, although to the right is the deep ravine of the narrow river, with small waterfalls. To the left can be seen the head of Stickle Valley which we climbed up an hour ago. Also to the left of our path is the rocky outcrop of Pike How, a wonderful viewpoint (8). The path soon becomes a stony man-made path, evidence of some skilled but very hard work, using local material. In places it is almost like a staircase, as it meanders steeply down towards the main valley below. Views are still glorious. The path coming down on the other side of the Ghyll can be clearly seen.

Lower down pass Dungeon Ghyll Force on our right, and in the steep valley notice a few trees growing in the sheltered ravine – holly or rowan – as we descend to a high stile and continue on down, with a wall on our left. Reach a gate and turn left, for a final stretch back to our starting point.

May

St Bees

This is a scenic walk for nature lovers, passing one of the most famous breeding cliffs for sea birds, as well as coastal and inland countryside where wild flowers grow in abundance. The village itself is an attractive settlement in the heart of the red sandstone which occurs both in this area and also in the far east of the Lake District around the Eden Valley.

Length: 7 miles

Time required: 3-4 hours but much more if bird watching delays your progress. Remember to take binoculars with you.

Terrain: a steep climb on to the cliffs but otherwise all quite gentle along clear paths or tracks.

Map: O.S. 1:25,000 Pathfinder 593, Whitehaven and St Bees.

Starting point: St Bees village or at the large car park near the beach, grid ref. 962118. St Bees is reached along the B5345 which comes off the A595 just south of Whitehaven. Regular trains along the Cumbria coastal railway which opened in 1848, stop at St Bees, and a bus service links St Bees with Whitehaven.

Facilities: St Bees village and at the beach. Nearest Tourist Information Centres are at Whitehaven (01946 852939) and Egremont (01946 820693).

Weather

As with every month, the relief of the Lake District produces big variations in the weather conditions experienced in two places only a few miles apart. The western coastal areas are influenced by the prevailing weather direction, but have their own distinctive features caused by the mildness and the dampness resulting from oceanic influences. Sea temperatures are still only about 10°C, but can be warming, especially if compared with winds from the east which can be very chilly, and Siberian. The St Bees coastline is often windy (or very windy), especially on the cliff tops, but can have high sunshine totals when mobile weather systems (and their rain) pass over quickly. May is often a good month for sunshine and also for good views, as the hotter days later in the year are often hazy, restricting the views across hill tops. Best views are often during northerly weather which often occurs in May, and can bring snow showers to the hills, but longer hours of daylight and increased warmth from the sun make this short lived. In 1998 the first week of the month was very changeable, but high pressure from Scandinavia dominated the weather in the middle of the month, with north east winds, giving dry but sunny weather; day maxima ranged from 17-24°C. This fine weather was ideal for helping the nesting season. The first and last weeks of the month were cloudier with some light rain, and maxima were lower, with 10-15° in the first week but up to 17 or 18° in the final week. Whatever the vagaries of the weather, spring has definitely sprung by the end of May, the third and last of the spring months.

The countryside

The month is named after Maia the Greek goddess who was one of the Pleiades, the seven daughters of Atlas, and was the mother of Hermes.

Mist in May, heat in June,
Makes the harvest come right soon.

This old saying has the sound of northern dialect about it, but mists in May will only give heat in June if settled anticyclonic weather causing the May mists continues into June, and such a prolonged spell of settled weather is rather unlikely. If harvests are referring to cereals, then these are not as common as in Wordsworth's time, when many fields of cereals could be seen in the Lake District. Around St Bees most of the farming is pastoral, with good grass growing in the maritime climatic conditions, supporting a few herds of cattle, but larger numbers of sheep. The lambs are growing up and

Guillemots on the cliffs

have gone beyond the cuddly stage. A few fields of barley were seen on this walk, and these interrupt what is generally a grassy landscape, and also interrupt bird life, as the use of chemicals reduces the amount of food for the birds and hence reduces the number of insect eating birds such as skylarks. However, land birds are numerous even in this coastal area, with summer visitors adding to the numbers of the residents. But, also moving into the area for the breeding season are the thousands of sea birds which come in to nest on the St Bees cliffs, one of the most popular cliff breeding grounds in England. The cliffs are rich in flowers as well as birds. Shrubs and trees thrive in the inland sections of the walk notably in the Rottington valley. Most trees are showing their full greenery by the end of the month, with the possible exception of the ash.

St Bees

The village is a small coastal resort near the most westerly point of Cumbria on St Bees Head, and the name is derived from an Irish princess, St Bee or St Bega, who founded a nunnery in about AD650. This became a Benedictine Priory in the 12th century, and the church of St Mary and St Bega was the church of the Priory, but has been much changed and restored, over the centuries. The impressive red sandstone church is set in the midst of lovely trees in the churchyard. The central tower was changed by Butterfield in the 19th century (from 1855-1858), when there were also changes in the north transept which saw the addition of the unusual wrought iron screen between the nave and chancel. There is only a small high

At Bees beach

window at the east end of the church, and three interesting windows at the west end set deep in the very thick walls. A carving of St Michael fighting a dragon in the churchyard wall opposite the west door is of special interest, as it dates from the 8th century. The Norman arch over the west door is the oldest feature of the Priory church (about 1160), and is magnificent, with its three orders of columns and zigzag ornament on the arch.

One of the major buildings in the village is the Public School which is also a large employer. It was founded as a grammar school in the 16th century by Archbishop Grindal, who unusually and remarkably refused to obey an order from Queen Elizabeth. He refused to restrict preaching meetings, as instructed, so she placed him under house arrest and he died in disgrace. However, on his deathbed in 1583, he founded St Bees School in the village of his birth. The original schoolhouse was built in 1587, and on the lintel stone of the original doorway can be seen the school motto "Ingredere ut proficias" (Come in and get on). The school is set round a central courtyard, which includes part of the 16th century buildings. The rest were added from 1842-44.

New Red Sandstone

The local red sandstone is used in several houses in St Bees, as well as in the school and church. Parts of the Lake District are fringed by red sandstone, most notably in the Vale of Eden and near to St Bees. These are the New Red Sandstones (Permian and Triassic times) when this area was located in the middle of a large continent and was experiencing a desert type of climate. Salt deposits have been found in these sandstones, a relic of the desert condition and these have contributed to chemical industries in Whitehaven, just to the north of St Bees. The sandstone

St Bees church door

rocks which form St Bees Head have been widely used as building stone, and not only in the local villages.

The Walk

Start from the village and walk to the beach (1), or use the large parking area by the beach, which is shingle at high tide but reveals lovely sand when the tide retreats. A few houses and a large caravan site are close to the beach, but the old village is half a mile inland. At the northern end of the beach is the Lifeboat Station and a notice to say this is the beginning of the Coast to Coast walk, devised by Alfred Wainwright. We are only doing 7 miles, not the 190 to Robin Hood's Bay – 3 hours rather than 3 weeks.

Cross the footbridge over Rottington Beck to reach the cliff path, which is stepped at first. Climb up steadily with views along the coast to the south improving at every step. The path is lined with colourful flowers, sea pinks, sea campion, yarrow, bluebells as well

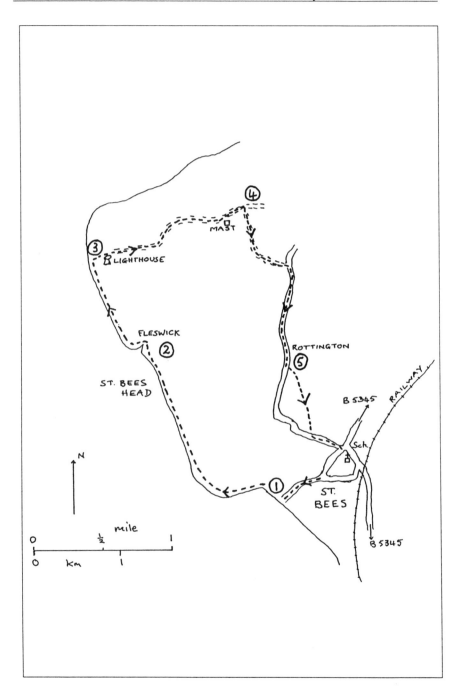

as gorse and bracken. There are lush green fields on the inland side of the path. Jackdaws and starlings are numerous, pipits and sky-larks are likely to be singing, and herring gulls will be lazily drifting by, noisily making their laughing call. From these cliff tops, which reach a height of 300ft (100m), the Isle of Man will be visible out to sea on a clear day. Swallows and house martins are likely to be con-stant companions, as well as sand martins, which nest on the cliffs to the left of the path in the early part of the walk.

Heading westwards at first, the cliff soon bends round towards the north west to pass the land slip area of Pattering Holes. Keep walking along the cliff top and after a couple of stiles and about 1½ miles, descend to Fleswick Bay where a steep valley has cut through the cliffs (2). Cross two stiles at the bottom and then on up the other side. This deep valley and a stony beach have had links with smug-glers in the past, who made use of a cave at the northern end of the beach. Erosion by the sea has worn away rocks to form a wave-cut platform and also enlarged joints in the sandstone to create small caves. The pebbly beach in the bay contains a variety of interesting and very smooth stones, including semi precious agate and jasper. Some of the pebbles are of glacial origin, having been deposited here by ice travelling from the north and several pebbles have been iden-tified as being from Scotland. Violets, primroses and celandines flourish in this sheltered valley, and amongst the land birds to be seen are willow warblers, whitethroats, linnets, stonechats and wheatears.

Once up on the cliff top again, we are now on St Bees Head, and soon reach special viewing points, for seeing cliffs, the sea and espe-cially the birds. The first viewing point will probably show nesting kittiwakes, fulmars, guillemots and gulls on the cliffs, possibly with a small number of black guillemots for which this is the only breed-ing site in England. Fulmars and herring gulls are often on the grassy ledges near the top. The second viewing point will reveal even larger numbers of guillemots as well as some razorbills, which are gener-ally on the lower ledges. Around here are a few puffins, but these are not always to be seen. Down on the sea also, will be many guille-mots, as well as a few cormorants and gulls. From there the Isle of Man is now back to the left, but straight out to sea is the Mull of Gal-loway, and the coast of Scotland, along the northern side of Solway Firth.

Continue along the cliff top, though now inside a fence, but on the edge of the cliffs may be seen more birds as well as pink campion, bluebells, stitchwort and celandines, typical hedgerows flowers thriving on this wild and windy cliff top.

Just before reaching the fog horn station **(3)**, turn right inland along a concrete track which leads to the left of the lighthouse, at 315ft (96m on the OS map). There has been a lighthouse here since 1717, but the present structure dates from 1866 and gives a light which can be seen 25 miles out to sea. Pass through a kissing gate and walk along the narrow road and contrast the surrounding fields with the view of Whitehaven ahead and to the left.

The road turns left through the farm complex of Tarnflatt Hall much of which is built of large red sandstone blocks, and the road turns right and then has a long straight with flower filled banks alongside. Note the windmills up the coast to the left. Pass a junction of tracks, with a mast, underground reservoir and meteorological station on the right. Keep straight on and go downhill slightly, and as the road levels and begins to bend right, turn right along a track **(4)**, with wall on left and hedge on right. More wild flowers line this track and small birds such as goldfinch, linnet and yellow hammer provide a constant twittering or song.

We reach a surfaced road and pass a few houses; notice the ferns growing by the bank and stream on the right as we go downhill again to join a larger road, though still quite narrow. Turn right. We pass a rookery, providing another variety of bird to add to a growing list seen on this walk. Vegetation is quite prolific on the roadside, and the variety of flowers now exceeds the variety of birds.

Pass a small nursery in a large sandstone house on the right, and a short woodland walk on the left, as we reach the hamlet of Rottington. Pass Whin Bank, the first house on the left, and then reach a footpath sign pointing up the driveway to the left between two large sandstone posts. Go along here **(5)**, and do not turn left over the bridge, but go left after the next building between a narrow stone stile and down some steps to a small rough field, through another stone pinch stile and into a riverside meadow. Keep straight ahead with the stream meandering to our left and then cross the stream over a footbridge. Immediately go right over a small footbridge and a stile and keep straight ahead along the right margin of the field. Follow this fence as it bends left, and look for the stile. Go right over the stile and diagonally across the middle of the field to the right of the telegraph pole mid-field, to reach a stile, and on across the next field just to the left of a telegraph pole to a stile and the road.

Turn left, and walk over the top of the hill and then descend towards St Bees. At the staggered crossroads, straight on is to the village if required, but otherwise turn right along Abbey Road. Good views of the church and the village can be seen to the left, and also the school cricket field. Pass Abbots Court on the right, formerly a hotel but now part of the school, and at the road junction turn right to walk back to the beach and the starting point.

June

Hawkshead

Hills, woods, lakes and hills all feature in this delightful walk, though the hills are not as high or as rugged as in the central Lake District. The views over Esthwaite and later over Windermere are magnificent.

Length: 10½ miles if the extension over Latterbarrow (800ft, 244m) is included or just under 9 miles if the shorter return route is followed.

Time required: 5 hours, or nearer 4 for the shorter version. Extra time will be necessary if a pub lunch is taken on the way or a visit to Hill Top is included.

Terrain: generally undulating with a couple of steep stretches, and possibility of muddy patches in the wooded areas.

Map: O.S. 1:25,000 Outdoor Leisure 7, The English Lakes South Eastern Area

Starting point: is in the car park at Hawkshead, GR354982 reached on the B5285 from Coniston or the Windermere-Bowness Ferry, or along the B5286 from Ambleside. Bus services from Ambleside and Coniston, the nearest small towns.

Facilities: Hawkshead has a Tourist Information Centre (01539436525) and a good selection of cafes and pubs.

___

Weather

The potential for variability in the weather is shown by an entry for 10th June in Dorothy Wordsworth's diary "cold showers with hail and rain … but after half past five the lake became calm and very beautiful". However the month can often be sunny and is the month of the summer solstice, which this year is on its normal date of 21st June, though can occasionally fall on the 20th or the 22nd. In the period before 1752 when the calendar was changed, the solstice came on the 10th June. This was because not enough leap years had been included during previous centuries, and the calendar was 11 days out. The Lake District in June 1998 saw daily maxima temperatures of only 12°C. in the middle of the month, though over 20°C. for a few days around the 20th. Rain fell on every day and there were some very wet days with more than half an inch and even over an inch on a few occasions. Old weather records have often shown that June had a strong westerly, and wet, spell in mid month and it was certainly true this year.

> *If St Vitus Day be rainy weather,*
> *It will rain for 30 days together.*

St Vitus Day is 15th June and although this old saying is not reliable and there is no reason why a rainy spell will continue for so long, it contained some truth this year.

The countryside

Swallows sit on the wires in Hawkshead village centre, house martins are also to be seen, and those other great insect chasers the swifts, are often screaming overhead, especially noticeable in the evenings. Out of the village, many small songbirds will be heard, and occasionally seen, in spite of all the greenery in which they seem able to disappear without trace. Warblers may be the most numerous birds in the hedges, but tits and a few goldcrests may be seen

Skylark

in the stands of larch and other conifers. Larger birds include crows and jackdaws, as well as jays which have the appropriate Latin name of *garrulus glandarius*, and they are certainly very garrulous. The predators such as kestrels, sparrow hawks and buzzards may also be seen as they search for food. Peregrines too will have chicks to feed and so are more in evidence than at other times of the year. For most birds this is a very busy month, with young requiring increasing and almost never ending amounts of food. The countryside is very green, not only because of the damp weather but also because most of the farmland is used as pasture. Cattle are more likely to be seen in the valleys than on the hillsides, and sheep are almost omnipresent. One of the most delightful noises of the fells is the constant calling of the lambs, now beginning to grow as large as their mothers. Mixed breeds are common, but there are still a few of the traditional Herdwick variety, whose survival was helped by the efforts of Beatrix Potter.

Hawkshead

This tiny town with its stone houses, narrow alleys and squares, and cobbled streets is a real mecca for tourists. There are hotels, cafes, bed and breakfast establishments, camping and caravan sites, as well as four pubs, one of which – The Red Lion – has two interesting figures just below the roof. One shows a farmer taking a pig to market, and the other is the man holding the whistle used to indicate the

One of Hawkshead's narrow lanes

beginning of sales. Dominating the village is the church of St Michael, on a small hill, and built of local Silurian rock with some St Bees sandstone for doorway and windows. It dates from the 16th and 17th centuries and has a low tower. The pillars supporting the arches inside the church vary in shape, being round or cylindrical on the north side, and roughly square on the south side. The paintings on the walls date from 1680 though some restoration and touching up work has been done on them. Adjacent to the church is the old grammar school founded in 1585 and later attended by William Wordsworth. The school was founded by Edwin Sandys, a local man who became Archbishop of York. The grammar school is now a museum, and Hawkshead is also the home of the Beatrix Potter Museum in "Bump or Bend" Cottage, the original offices of W.H. Heelis and Son. Hawkshead is a Norse foundation, named after the farm of Haukr, who built the original settlement. It is possible that the Norse brought the famous Herdwick sheep with them. Close to the church is Pillar House, with its flight of steps, one of many old houses which have a story to tell. Ann Tysons cottage is where Wordsworth lodged for a time whilst at the Grammar School, and the road nearby was called Rag, Putty and Leather Street, as two tailors, two painters and two cobblers lived there.

Hawkshead church

Sawrey

The two small villages of Far Sawrey and Near Sawrey are less than a mile apart, and each has a pub. Situated on the narrow main road from the ferry to Hawkshead, most tourists arrive by car, to visit these lovely stone villages set in beautiful surroundings. Far Sawrey has a fine church, dating from 1866-1872, and described by Pevsner as "a decent, honest piece of work", but the main attraction is Hill Top, the famous house of Beatrix Potter, now owned by the National Trust.

Mrs. William Heelis

Beatrix Potter was born in 1866, and grew to love the Lake District because of family holidays when she was a girl. From the age of 16 she came to the Lake District (previous holidays had always been in Scotland) for the annual three-month long holidays which were taken alongside Derwent Water from 1885 until 1903, and then near Esthwaite. Her first book to be published was Peter Rabbit, in 1902, followed by The Tailor of Gloucester and Squirrel Nutkin in 1903. Squirrel Nutkin, together with The Tale of Benjamin Bunny and Tale of Mrs. Tiggy Winkle were all set around Derwent Water. With money earned from her writing, she bought Hill Top in 1905 and several books were set in or near this farm. Tom Kitten, Samuel Whiskers and Jemima Puddle-duck all lived around this area. She gradually added to her purchases by buying more land and farms, and became a great protector of the landscape. Farms were restored and maintained and she encouraged the survival of the Herdwick breed of sheep. Having met Canon Hardwicke Rawnsley, one of the founders of the National Trust, who had become a friend of the family in the summer visits, she discussed several of her projects with him. Her interest in conservation resulted in her leaving all her land to the Trust. Beatrix Potter used the local firm of solicitors W.H. Heelis and Son for her property purchases and in 1913 she married William Heelis. For several years prior to her marriage, she was becoming more a farmer than a writer, and most of her books had all been written by the time she married, though *The Tale of Johnny Town Mouse*, based in Hawkshead was not published until 1918. She died in 1943.

Field Boundaries

Near Hawkshead field boundaries may be hedges, stone walls or vertical slabs of stone which are often referred to as Brathay Slabs, and are thin sheets of easily cleaved local slatey rock. These unusual field boundaries date from the time of the Enclosure Acts of the 18th century, and a few are thought to be even older. These older boundaries are from the 15th century, and were ecclesiastical boundaries. The sheets of rock up from 2-4 feet in height are sunk into the ground, and they make a sheep-proof fence.

The Walk

Leave the centre of Hawkshead (1) at the Tourist Information Centre and walk through the main car park, then turn left along the road. As the road begins to bend left, cross over to walk along a stony track which narrows into a path between a house on the left and the camping site on the right. Cross over the footbridge and through a gate into a pasture field. Turn left across the field, which is often damp and contains colourful marsh marigolds and ladies smock. Go through a kissing gate and then diagonally right across the next field, to reach another gate and turn right to follow the signpost to Colthouse. Go through a kissing gate and straight across Scar House Lane which is lined by banks rich in wild flowers. Pass through another gate and up the steep slope, then over a stone stile and diagonally left across the next field. This leads to a gap in a wall and (over to the right are the first views of Esthwaite Water) our path then passes a house and we turn left alongside the garden and beech hedge to reach a large wooden gate and then a stony driveway.

Turn right here for about 50m.to reach the road (2), and then left for about 70 metres, and just before the gated drive to Gillbank, turn sharp right through a gate and on to a bridleway signposted to Claife Heights. After 30-40 metres the track splits and we keep right (with a blue arrow) along a fairly level track, though it soon begins to climb steadily. This is a stony and rocky track, and as it climbs through an open grassy area with scattered trees (like parkland), wonderful views open up towards Hawkshead and the Coniston hills beyond. Cross a stream and keep ahead through a gate bordered by one of those distinctive stone slab field boundaries. Pass through another

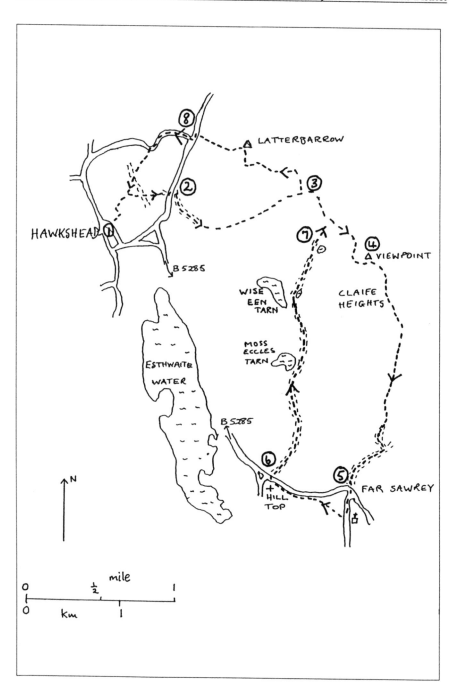

Redstart

open stretch, where redstarts may be seen, and keep climbing steadily, with several larch trees and a small stream on our right. Cross over a stream, with a small wetland habitat alongside it, and keep climbing steadily, passing a small grassy pond over the wall to the right, and the top of Latterbarrow Hill with its tall cairn is seen over to the left. Go through a gate and walk on, with conifers on both sides now, and out through a gate to reach the guide post **(3)**. We return to this point on the return journey, when the short cut or longer route will have to be chosen.

Follow the sign to Ferry and Far Sawrey going straight ahead, on the route marked by white posts. This is the clearly marked route from the Ferry and Ash Landing car park for three miles to Latterbarrow, and was created in 1966 by the National Park Authority, never exceeding a height of 245 metres. We are at post 11, and keep straight on to pass through an area of recent cutting (1998) but all of the forests are continually changing as areas are cut and new ones planted. At a major cross tracks (post 10) turn right towards Ferry and Far Sawrey and, at the next cross tracks (post 9) keep straight on, as far as the sharp right bend at post number 8. Here, we leave the track and bridleway to head straight on into the woods following the footpath to Ferry and Far Sawrey. Our path through the dark and gloomy evergreen woods (though cool on a hot day) is well worn and clearly marked by white-topped posts. There may be very damp areas even in June. Emerge from the woods to an open area of recent cutting (1998) at post 7, turn right and follow the path up to a large rock at the top with a wonderful viewpoint **(4)** along Windermere to Ambleside as well to all the surrounding hills, including the Langdale Pikes. The large rock makes a good picnic site, as it has been smoothed by ice. It is one of several hard rock outcrops in this woodland area, scraped over by the ice, but indicating that the soil around here is thin and not very rich, yet the trees manage to grow here.

From this wonderful viewpoint, follow the posts as the path meanders through the tree stumps, to reach a stony forestry track where we turn right, at post 6. Pass a small pool on the right, and then turn left at post 5, back into more dark woods. The difference between dark evergreen conifers and the more open broadleaved or larch woodland is clearly seen on this walk, with undergrowth, and singing birds in the lighter areas of woodland. A view down to Windermere and Belle Isle can be seen to our left, as we walk on through the woods, to post number 4. Belle Isle has had a varied history, as it contained a manor house until the 14th century, and was the site of a siege during the Civil War. The present roundhouse on the island dates from the 19th century. Keep straight on towards Far Sawrey, over rocks and tree roots – which are numerous on this path. To the left Bowness and the ferry may be seen, and distant views show the Pennines and the distinctive shape of Ingleborough, on a clear day.

As the wood opens out a little, more flowers may be seen. We pass a wooden bench, and soon reach a gate and emerge to a more open area and grassy fields. The path leads to a lane between stone walls, and descends to a T-junction of paths, with left turn to the Ferry (across the lake to Bowness), but we turn right through a gate towards Far Sawrey. Follow the track alongside a wall, and then through a gate and descend to the road where we turn right.

A few metres along the road is the Sawrey Hotel **(5)** with a bar at the far end, called the Claife Crier which is good for walkers, and serves excellent food, as well as refreshing liquid. Nearly opposite the hotel is a narrow road to the village store and the church, and we walk along here passing a few houses as far as the church where we turn right through a kissing gate to follow a path across fields. Part of the path is alongside a small stream where marsh marigolds may still be very colourful. After two fields the path leads between wire fences and runs alongside the road towards Hill Top and Near Sawrey.

Pass Hill Top on the left and then the Tower Bank Arms, also owned by the National Trust. A few metres further along the road **(6)**, turn right along a narrow road. The first house on the left is Anvil Cottage and note the anvil in a recess above the door. Follow this road which becomes a stony track, and climb away from the village. Pass a gate or over the stile alongside as we pass a large barn, and are joined by a track from the right, coming up from Far Sawrey. The clear track continues to climb steadily and soon reaches the idyllic

Moss Eccles Tarn, where fishermen may be sitting quietly on the bank, and the ducks and swans will be sitting on eggs or feeding their young at this time of year. Beatrix and William used to enjoy rowing on this lake, and she would draw whilst he fished.

Continue to climb gradually, and pass through a gate to reach two more tarns (to our left is Wise Een Tarn), with wonderful views of Langdale ahead. The larger lake to our left may have lapwings and black headed gulls as well as a few ducks and geese. The track descends slightly as it passes between the lakes, and then climbs again, in an area with larch trees, still looking fresh and light green in June, and with grass growing beneath.

Walk on through a gate and a coniferous area, though with a few larch to lighten the appearance of the woodland. This is red squirrel territory. Pass a small lake to the right, and after a horizontal stretch of walking, where the gravel track goes steeply down and bends right, we go left along a stony bridleway (7) descending quite steeply through trees. At a major cross paths we turn left at post number 9, and we are retracing steps along our outward route.

The track descends and then rises to a major cross tracks where we turn left at post 10, and on to a gate with post number 11, which is the time of decision (3 again). Here the walk back to Hawkshead can simply retrace steps of the outward journey, or to add an extra mile and a half, it is possible to turn right and reach Hawkshead via the top of Latterbarrow.

Short cut

Just retrace steps of the outward walk, following the clear track until it meets the narrow road, then turn left and follow this road back into Hawkshead.

Longer walk

Turn right at post 11, with its white top, and the path soon begins to descend, with trees on the left, but a recently cleared area over the wall to the right. Pass some very smooth ice scraped rocks and descend to the next white topped post, then the path levels for a few metres. Climb again, a short steep ascent to a wall, then turn right, passing more white topped posts, on a clear path through the trees. This is a very sheltered stretch, as we descend slightly to a footbridge in a damp hollow, still following the white-topped posts. Walk along the path, now close to the margin of the woods on our right, and reach a stile and post number 12.

Go right over this stile and the path divides, left along the wall to Hawkshead and right up the hillside to the cairn on the top of Latterbarrow. We go right, on the grassy path through the bracken, and we may find the wind increasing and feeling refreshing on this exposed hillside, with wonderful all round views, including the Langdale Pikes, the mast in Grizedale Forest, and Ambleside at the northern end of the lake.

Turn left from the tall cairn and follow a grassy path through bracken and heading steeply downhill – in the direction of Hawkshead. Go down to the trees and before reaching the wall, bend right, along a narrow path following the wall and slowly descending, before going more steeply across a field. At the bottom of the field is the National Trust sign for Latterbarrow and we go through the gate and turn left along the road **(8)**. After only a few metres the road divides and we turn right along a narrow road between hazel hedges, with stone slabs on the left side. Pass through a small wood and continue along the road, and as the road bends sharply to the right, just before the farm buildings, there are two paths on the left.

Take the second of these, through a kissing gate by a large wooden gate, and follow the signpost to Hawkshead. Walk along the right side of the field to reach a gate, and through this turn left to continue along the left side of this next field. After another stile and gate, walk along the left side of another field to reach a kissing gate and Scar House Lane. Turn left along the lane for about 40 metres and then go right through a kissing gate with wooden gate but two large slabs of rock as gate posts, and go diagonally left across the next field, over a stile and across another field, to a kissing gate where we rejoin the route of our outward journey. Go through the gate and head diagonally left across a damp field to return to Hawkshead.

July

Haweswater and High Street

This walk reaches the highest point of any of the 12 walks in this book, taking us up a steep climb, and ending with a steep descent. In between is the skyline walk along High Street with a panoramic view across the entire Lake District. As with all walks the distance measured on the map cannot take into consideration the winding paths and the ups and downs. This is a harder walk than the bald mileage distance would suggest.

Length: 9 miles with a short cut option of 7½ miles.

Time required: 6 hours, or 4 for the short cut.

Terrain: gentle in the valley but a steep climb and ascent to and from High Street, which itself is quite gentle but weather can be hostile here, even in mid summer.

Map: O.S. 1:25,000 Outdoor Leisure number 5, the North Eastern Area of the English Lakes.

Starting point: Mardale Head GR469107, reached on the B road which runs from Bampton along the eastern side of Haweswater. A bus service runs from Penrith to Bampton, and at weekends and Bank Holidays the Haweswater Rambler runs from Penrith to the end of the Mardale road.

Facilities: Nearest refreshment is at the Haweswater Hotel or at Bampton. Nearest Tourist Information Centre is at Penrith (01768 867466)

Weather

In this area as much as any in the Lake District the differences between the hill top and the valley may be noticed, both in the amounts of cloud and rain, but also in the wind and exposure. Average temperatures decrease with height, and rainfall increases with height, giving considerable variations over short distances. The average rainfall over the catchment area of Haweswater is said to be 1870mm per annum (75 inches) but some of the hill areas will undoubtedly receive more than 2500mm (100 inches). Rain is frequent even in the summer months, and this year turned out to be wetter than average. Low pressure and associated fronts were common, and several days (e.g. 17th and 26th) were very wet, though the worst was the weekend of the 12th when a depression, very deep for the summer months, passed overhead. Associated with the cloud and rain, temperatures were rather low, daily maxima rarely reaching 20°C, and the sunniest weather occurred early in the month whilst north-westerly winds were blowing. St Swithin's Day (15th) was one of the driest in the month, though most of the following days experienced some rain.

'The English winter ends in July and recommences in August', wrote Byron in 'Don Juan', and this gloomy assessment seemed very relevant in 1998.

The countryside

The countryside looked much greener than in an average July, as three wet months in the last four, with no prolonged hot spells, ensured that vegetation remained very lush. The Lake District was magnificent in all its varying shades of greenery, the lakes had high water levels, and many streams and waterfalls were at their best and most impressive, all adding to the beauties of the scenery. The farms were full of grazing sheep, with the lambs almost as large as their parents. Those which are Herdwick will have lost most of the black colouring they have as lambs, as they become lighter with maturity. Their calls were to be heard all day and every day, echoing across the valleys.

Wild flowers are abundant on verges and include meadow sweet and wild geranium, as well as buttercups, foxgloves and the beginnings of the ragwort season. Harebells can be seen along roadsides as well as out on the windswept fells where they survive in spite of looking delicate and fragile. In the valleys trees are still very green, but fruits are appearing; ash trees have new keys; the lime have flowers; and some hawthorn have green berries. Bracken is growing well, and is now spreading across many of the paths. Bird life is abundant, and many parents are busy feeding young, but out of the nest now, as the young are fully grown - but still looking fluffy and often paler than parents. Many of the young birds are tamer and more approachable than the parents, as they have yet to learn fear, or common sense. Even up on the fells the birds have young, although raven and dipper have finished, and the Riggindale eagles had no success this year. Robin, pied wagtail, pied flycatchers, spotted flycatcher are all likely to be seen feeding young in mid July. Swallows too may be seen feeding their young, which sit on stone walls, rather than on telegraph wires which would normally be used in more populated areas. Rocky areas and stone walls may have their pied wagtails, ring ouzels and wheatears. This last is an especially thoughtful bird, kind to the bird watcher, as it makes the noise of chinking stones which can be easily heard, and recognised, and when it flies it shows its white rump which is easily seen. As you look around the hillsides you may see a small herd of wild fell ponies on the slopes above Blea Tarn, and everywhere there will be sheep, even on the top of High Street. One of the major objections to the creation of the Haweswater reservoir was the effect it would have on wild life. Perhaps surprisingly, some wild life has been helped by the creation of the larger lake with the habitat for water birds. The increased isolation and quietness of the valley, with no resident humans, may also have helped to create a wilder environment - which suits some creatures, notably the golden eagle and the red deer.

Haweswater

Manchester had been using water from the reservoir created by the Corporation at Thirlmere since the end of the 19th century, but greater demand made them look for increased supplies from the Lake District. Haweswater was chosen because it was the highest lake in the Lake District, at 694ft (212m) which was useful when transferring the water nearly 100 miles to the south. Top water level now is at a height of 790ft(241m) above sea level. The lake which already existed was enlarged as a result of the dam built by Manchester Corporation which acquired Haweswater by Act of Parliament in 1919. Work started in 1930 and the dam was completed in 1941, making Haweswater 4½ miles in length and raising the water level by 90ft (27m). The original lake had been about 2½ miles in length. In the drought of 1984, the reservoir was falling at the rate of 3ft per week, and to replace about 80 million gallons drawn out each day, less than one million were flowing in.

Mardale Beck flowing towards Haweswater

Haweswater Hotel

The village of Mardale (meaning valley with a lake) was flooded by the creation of the reservoir, and Manchester Corporation was required to build a pub/hotel to replace the Dun Bull Inn in Mardale. Located half way along the road which follows the east side of the lake, this hotel was built in 1937 by Manchester Corporation, for the use of visitors. It was also used by members of the corporation for meetings or for mini weekend breaks. The council sold the hotel in the mid 1980s after which it deteriorated and became very run down. Restored to some of its former grandeur by the present owner, this magnificent building is in a wonderful setting, one of the most dramatic and impressive in the entire Lake District. Most windows give views across to the fells on the west side of the lake, and some also reveal the view south to the end of the valley, with Riggindale backed by High Street. The terraced garden also overlooks the lake. The hotel is highly recommended for a comfortable break in a friendly atmosphere and with excellent food. It is built of local stone and with a roof of Cumberland slate taken from the roofs of the old farm buildings in Mardale.

Mardale village

Before flooding of this village took place the houses were blown up but Holy Trinity church was taken down stone by stone and these were taken to other churches, and some were used to build the reservoir tower where the drawing off of water is controlled. The graves were exhumed and many bodies were reburied at Shap church. The small school was also taken down carefully and rebuilt at Walmgate Head and is now a private residence. The shapes of the walls sometimes appear in times of low water (but certainly not this year –

Looking along Haweswater, over the former site of Mardale village

1998!!) as happened in 1976, 1984 and last seen in 1995, when the lake level was reduced by 26%. Large numbers of visitors came in to see the village remains, leaving litter and taking stones as souvenirs! Sheep farming was the main way of life for the inhabitants of Mardale, and the valley is still used in the same way. The annual autumn shepherd's meet was originally held up on High Street, but in recent times were held near the Dun Bull Inn. The annual meet is now held in Bampton.

Golden eagle

There are an estimated 425 pairs of golden eagles in Scotland, none in Wales and just one pair in Riggindale. This is the only location for nesting golden eagles in England and there has been a pair here since the 1960s. It has not been the same pair throughout this time, as when one of the pair disappears or dies, the remaining bird seems to find a new mate, and returns to Riggindale to nest. There have been three females and two males. The new mate probably comes from the south of Scotland, the nearest location where other eagles nest, but little is known for certain about the origin of these birds,

Golden Eagle with chick

and little is also known about what happens to the young eagles which have been reared here. Sadly the 1998 nesting season was unsuccessful with only one egg laid and this did not hatch. If the eggs do not hatch by 45th day they are taken out to be investigated to find reasons for non hatching.

The walk

Leave the car park **(1)**, and at the end of the road go through the gate where there may be a notice about red deer calving in June. Walk alongside the wall to where it turns right and there is a three way

The tower in the reservoir

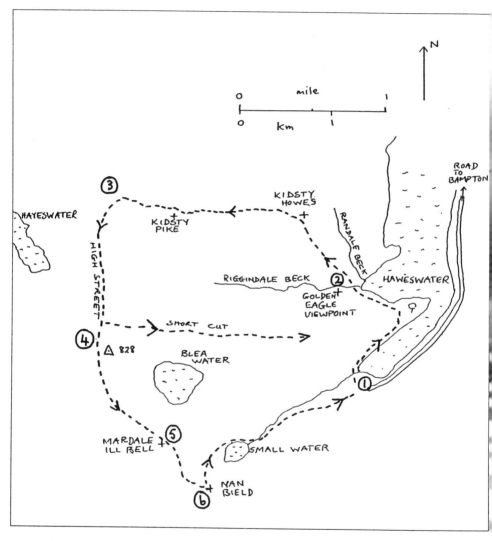

split of the path, left towards Gatescarth Pass and Longsleddale, straight ahead to Small Water, Nan Bield Pass and Kentmere and right to Bampton. An RSPB notice gives a map and probably the information that the eagle viewing point is open (from 9am till 5pm daily). We turn right alongside the wall with the noise of sheep and tumbling streams all around us, and a dramatic head of valley to our left. Cross the bridge over the Mardale Beck, and then turn right along the side of the lake. Pied wagtails will almost certainly be in evidence and keep a careful look out for sight or sound of the common sandpiper along the lake margin.

The path moves left away from the lake along the edge of the woodland. At the top of this slight climb, a path goes off to the left, to climb up the ridge to Riggindale Crag (the route for the short cut return if required), but we keep ahead, with new views of the lake to our right. On the lake will be screaming gulls especially near the small island of Wood Howe, Canada geese, a few ducks, cormorants, great crested grebes (which spend the summer here but do not nest), mergansers and goosanders. Near the lake margin can be seen the stone walls round the former fields used by the villagers of Mardale, before flooding occurred.

The path heads towards a small patch of woodland and is lined with rocks stuck vertically in the ground marking the path leading to the bridge (2) across the beck. Before going over the bridge, bear left to walk up the valley passing a stone building and alongside a wall, to visit the RSPB hut and viewpoint in the hope of seeing one or both of the pair of eagles. The valley also contains nesting ring ouzels, red deer (and at this time of the year the new calves are nearly fully grown but still showing some of their youthful spotty marking) and stoats.

Retrace steps to the path lined with short vertical stones, and cross over Riggindale Beck, which will have a powerful flow if the recent weather has been wet (which it normally will have been). The path then splits and the right fork goes over Randale Beck and along the lake side, but we turn left to begin the hard climb.

Be prepared for a change in the weather, as it will certainly be much windier and cooler up on the top, and of course cloud and rain can always move in to affect the tops of the hills. Although the hills are a source of pleasure and enjoyment, they can still be dangerous and must be treated with respect.

The path is slightly worn as it meanders up through a grassy area and is easy to follow, and the steep climb reveals new views every few minutes, as more of Riggindale and Haweswater can be seen. We climb on through a rocky area, Kidsty Howes, and in places the path has been made with stones, where erosion has caused gullying. Several rocks with patches or strips of the bright white mineral quartz will be seen. Climb up through the Howes to reach a less steep section, as views beyond Haweswater open up to reveal the Pennines. In addition to pipits there may be wheatears along this stretch, feeding their young, and possibly skylarks singing overhead. The sharp peak of Kidsty Pike 2560ft (780m) comes into sight, and the path goes over this or follows small cairns to pass to the right of it, as the climb continues, still heading west. We can now see the deep Randale valley to the right and the deeper Riggindale down to the left, with High Street stretching away beyond the top of Riggindale. Keep looking out over Riggindale in case one of the eagles has taken to the air.

As the climb continues, a path comes in from the right (3) as we bend to the left to become south-westerly in direction, and shortly we reach the well worn and stony path along the top of High Street. We turn left here and head southwards, going downhill, which is a pleasant change, on the ridge which is very narrow here – called the Straits of Riggindale. Follow the wall on our right and then the path goes through to the other side of the wall as we head towards the next climb on the path clearly visible ahead, which is the route of the old Roman road.

The wall, now on our left, is a good aid to navigation in poor visibility, though the path diverges to the right, near the edge of the steep slope down to Hayeswater. As the path climbs steadily up to the highest point of High Street, the 4.3m (14ft) high beacon (looking like a large trig point) on Thornthwaite Crag can be clearly seen, but we are forking left long before reaching there. It is probably better at this point to walk not along this clear path, but alongside the wall, with goods view out to the left. Just before reaching the triangulation point (4), note the cairn at the top of the path leading down on to Riggindale Crag, as this is a slight short cut return journey if required (7½ miles instead of nearly 9 for the longer way back). If returning by this route, the first part is steeply down the rocky slope called Long Stile and at the grassy depression (called Caspel Gate) where there is a small lake except in dry spells of weather, there is a decision to be made. The choice is either keeping along the ridge of Rough Crag, (which is clear and easy to follow although beware there are steep slopes on both sides), or descending right down to Blea Tarn. If taking the path down to this corrie lake, (the name is from the Norse for black lake), pass the left end of the tarn and thence down Blea Water Beck back to the car parking place at the end of Haweswater.

If going on for the main route, follow the wall to reach the triangulation point, at a height of 2717ft (828m) with, on a clear day, wonderful all round views to hill after hill, including Helvellyn away to the right. The fairly flat area around here is known as Racecourse Hill, for historical reasons. Local shepherds and farmers used this area for races and fairs in former times, and much earlier than that, the Romans marched along here, between their garrisons at Windermere and Brougham. There are still likely to be sheep grazing up here, whatever the weather, and they all tend to face downwind, turning their backsides into the wind.

Continue alongside the wall in a southerly direction (bearing of about 190° and just after the wall has a slight change of direction to more southwesterly (bearing about 210°), take the path going off left (170° or 160° and then south easterly) towards Mardale Ill Bell about half a mile distant. To the left of our path is the very steep back wall of the corrie containing Blea Water, and our route follows closely to the top edge of this steep slope. An alternative route from the top of High Street is to stay close to the wall and follow it as far as the point where it turns sharp right, and here we go left through a gap in the wall, and follow a path across the peaty area in an easterly direction. This will take us to merge with the previously mentioned path just before reaching the cairns on the top of Mardale Ill Bell **(5)**. Down to the north from this peak is Blea Water, the deepest tarn in the Lake District with a depth of 207ft (63 metres).

From Mardale Ill Bell follow the worn and stony path heading southwards (160 bearing) and then south eastwards, towards Nan Bield Pass. This path is often steep in places and then more gentle but is a continuous descent, with views left down to Small Water, where we are heading, and right down to Kentmere Reservoir and valley. At Nan Bield **(6)** we reach a stone wind shelter, where we turn left, to continue even more steeply along the rocky path down to Small Water. In rainy weather, here as elsewhere in the Lakes, the easiest route for water is often along the worn route of the footpath, so it can be wet on our downhill route. The steep and meandering path leads down to the lake and alongside the lake pass the 3 small stone shelters, evidence of the former importance of this path as a routeway, possibly even as a trade route in former centuries. Just past these shelters notice several large rocks perched or overhanging, as though they had fallen down the slope or been dropped by ice, and come to rest against an obstacle. Small Water is a perched corrie as it hangs over the lower part of its valley.

At the far end of the lake the path crosses the outflow (with difficulty after heavy rain) and continues down the right side of Small Water Beck, passing several waterfalls. These are impressive after rain – one consolation of experiencing rain on this walk is that the streams and waterfalls are all more picturesque. As the path begins to level off, notice all the hummocky piles of debris deposited here by ice, probably at the time of the last ice advance in the Ice Age, about 12,000 years ago. This path leads past these morainic mounds down to the road, and car park where we began a few hours ago.

August

Boot and Hardknott

Visiting the far west of the Lake District to explore the beautiful Esk Valley, we walk upstream to the dramatic Roman fort set in the wild landscape of Hardknott Pass.

Length: 8 miles

Time required: about 4 hours

Terrain: often wet and muddy, and part of the path alongside the Esk is rocky. There is a steep climb up to Hardknott and a corresponding steep descent to Brotherilkeld.

Map: O.S. 1:25,000 Outdoor Leisure map number 6, the Lake District South West.

Starting point: Boot, GR173007, which is reached by the narrow road leading from the A595 near Ravenglass, or by the narrow gauge Ravenglass Railway.

Facilities: The nearest small town is Seascale and the nearest Tourist Information Centre is at Egremont (01946 820693). Refreshments are available at pubs in Boot and Eskdale Green.

Weather

August is often one of the wettest months of the year, and 1998 was no exception with a mostly dull and rainy month caused by a series of depressions passing from the west, centred over Scotland but extending their influence into north west England. Low pressure systems are always more likely than in the two previous months, as there is little Arctic high pressure to block the passage of these depressions. There was some rain on most days, and the wettest of all was the 2nd when up to 2 inches fell is several localities. Most days were showery, and the driest spell of the month was from the 27th till the 31st, when touches of autumn were seen, with chilly and misty nights. Maximum daily temperatures were generally below 20°C., only exceeding that figure for a few days after the 9th and then again near the end of the month. During the last few days of the month, when higher pressure was prevailing, the days became hazy and therefore views from hilltops were restricted.

The old saying that St Bartholomew's Day (24th August) brings the dew, and introduces autumnal conditions nearly had some truth this year, as dew and mist were experienced three days later. St Bartholomew is also expected to conclude the 40-day spell of weather since St Swithun's Day.

The countryside

Many of the flowers so colourful in July can still be seen, though they are beginning to fade. Ragwort has been particularly widespread and with increasing publicity about the danger of this plant which is poisonous to horses if included in hay, many attempts were made to remove it from meadows and roadsides. These have included a special ragwort week, and a sample scheme being implemented in part of Shropshire in an attempt to eradicate it. Bracken has continued to grow and is often spreading across paths.

Spotted flycatcher (left) and wheatear

Most of the birds which have been feeding their young in July are still in family groups at the beginning of the month, but towards the end the families are splitting up and many of the summer visitors are moving southwards to begin their migration. Pipits and wheatears may still by seen on the fells, and pied wagtails are common in the valleys, flittering along the stone walls where they may have nested, or following sheep or cattle which disturb insects in the grass. Swallows will be around the farms at the beginning of the month and may be congregating on wires, or on walls if no wires are available, before beginning their migration. As the days shorten towards the end of the month, most of the summer-visiting flycatchers will have departed too. The first of the winter visitors, the waders from Scandinavia and the Arctic regions will be arriving, though not to stay in one place, but just to rest before moving on further south. The resident grouse will still be around, unless the activities on the 12th August have made much impact on their numbers.

The countryside has remained very green this year, because of the weather conditions experienced, though expanses of pink survive on roadside where rose bay willow herb has been growing. The fluffy seeds are likely to be drifting around like small snowstorms whenever the wind blows strongly. Other wild flowers are also still showing colour on the roadside verges, and the dainty and delicate looking harebells will be waving in the winds on the hillsides.

Although this is the main holiday month, this part of the Lake District is likely to be fairly quiet especially in mid-week, and country walks can give solitude if required or desired.

Eskdale

The valley has a history of water powered mills, for corn and for making bobbins, and the 16th century corn mill in Boot has been restored as a museum. This mill ground corn until the 1920s and the upper wheel of the mill made electricity until 1955 when power lines brought mains electricity to this area. Renovation work in the 1970s enabled the mill to carry on working. At the rear of the mill is the turbulent stream with waterfalls which provide the head of water to turn two huge wheels.

The picturesque valley has also been involved in mining and a 3ft (914mm) gauge railway line was built to link the main line at

Ravenglass to Boot in 1875. Known locally as L'al Ratty, after a Mr Ratcliffe, the Ravenglass and Eskdale Railway was never very profitable and it closed in 1913, to be replaced the next year by the even narrower 15 inch (381mm) gauge. This was used for carrying granite from the quarries as well as passengers but, when the granite quarries closed in 1953, it could not survive on the tourist traffic available at that time. However, it was bought by a group of enthusiasts in 1960 and is now operated by a company, so the Ravenglass and Eskdale railway survives. Trains run throughout most of the year, though with only a very limited service in the winter.

On the Ravenglass and Eskdale Railway

Boot

The small village was involved in mining and the light railway mentioned above was built to transport haematite from the Nab Scar mine, but the mine was not very productive. There was also peat cutting on the hills nearby, and there are still remains of granite huts to the north of the village on Boot Bank, which were used for storing peat, especially in the 18th century but still in use into the 1920s. Boot was also important for milling because of the fast stream. The name Boot is derived from Old English for a bend in the river. An old

Spring

Borrowdale

Tarn Hows

Summer

Brantwood

St Bees

Autumn

Ravenglass & Eskdale Railway

Coniston

Winter

The Langdale Pikes

Derwent Water

packhorse bridge across the river leads up to Boot Bank, and this was the route to several tracks, including the corpse trail bringing bodies over the hills from Wasdale where there was no church or burial ground. Adjacent to the bridge is the old mill, now a working museum, and also adjacent to it is the location of the end of the old railway line. The village contains a pub, a shop and a few cottages, now for holiday visitors but formerly the homes of miners. Dalegarth station, the terminus of the Ravenglass and Eskdale railway is just along the road from the village.

St Catherine's church

This delightful church is built of pink granite and red sandstone, and the gravestones are of many other types of rock too. It appears to be hidden away, but was the burial ground for Wasdale as well as Eskdale. One of the most famous memorials in the churchyard is to Thomas Dobson, a legendary huntsman of the Eskdale and Ennerdale pack. House martins often nest in the entrance porch. The church is a typical dale chapel, a low building, with nave and chancel all in one. It has an octagonal font, which is known to have spent 60 years lying in the farmyard at Kirk House. Little is known of

St Catherine's church

the early history of this church, although the present church is thought to have been built of local rock in the 17th century and dedicated to St Catherine, the patron saint of soldiers. More definite information records that in a major restoration in 1881, much of the church was rebuilt.

Hardknott Castle

There are gates in the middle of each of the four walls. An information board near the main gate (the south gate) tells a little of the history of this remarkable fort, named Mediobogdum, which is located on a spur between Eskdale and Hardknott Gill, in a site as dramatic as any fort anywhere in the Roman Empire. The fort is nearly square and covers 3 acres (1.2 hectares), and was built during the reign of Hadrian (AD118-138) on the route from Ambleside to Ravenglass, and was garrisoned by the 4th cohort of Dalmatians. It was only occupied for a short time and little used after the end of the 2nd century. Inside the fort can be seen remains of the main buildings, including the Commanders house and store room, which were built of stone. It probably housed about 500 men, but the living quarters were of wood and little evidence remains. There are baths outside the stone wall, between the fort and the road, and to the north east is

Hardknott Roman fort

an artificially smoothed area which is thought to have been the parade ground. A rocky outcrop at the northern edge may have been used by the commander for surveying the troops. Another small gate looks out north, towards Scafell. Near the west gate, an information board tells us that the wall below the narrow slate course is the original Roman wall, which has been treated to prevent collapse. Above the slate the wall has been reconstructed from fallen Roman facing stones to a height of not more than 6'6" (1.9m), which was the maximum height of the original walls.

Geology

The Eskdale granite is an intrusion covering about 35 square miles, but coming up from a much larger area of granite (a batholith) at depth, and dating from about 400 million years ago. The granite in the area around Boot is often pink in colour, and is generally coarse grained and individual minerals in the rock can be seen. Many buildings have been made from this rock and stone walls are numerous. These are often very wide, because of the large number of loose rocks which had been lying around in the fields. Many of the rocks are smooth and rounded, evidence that they were probably on the bed of a stream for many years. Another rock, to be seen in some of the buildings, is the reddish sandstone from the coastal areas near St Bees. This is more easily cut and shaped than the local granite and is used for the surrounds of doors and windows.

The Walk

Walk along the road (1) from the station (or from the village), and take the lane opposite Brook House Inn, signposted to the church. Pass a few houses on this track, including fine granite buildings, many other examples of which can be seen in this area, where the pinkish granites are found. Kirk House is the last house on the right and opposite this is a stone barn, where swallows nest. Then the lane leads on to the church (2) and the river, with its stepping stones. The church and churchyard are well worth a visit.

For the onward walk either cross the stepping stones and follow the path bending round to the left to walk upstream to Gill Force bridge, or, as there is no need to cross the river, just turn left along

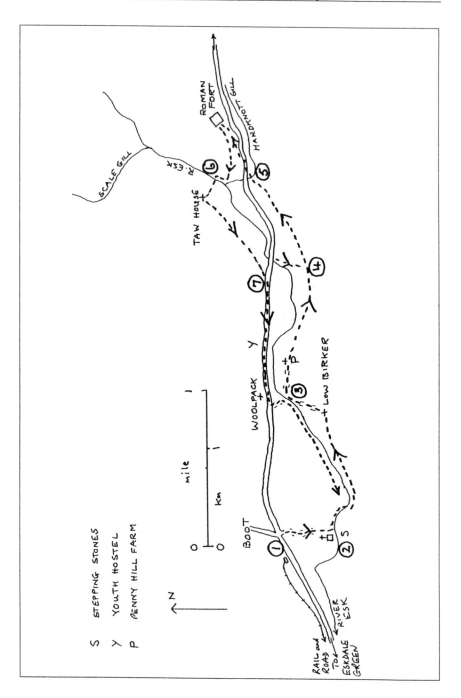

the river bank. This walk is signposted to Doctor's Bridge and Gill Force Bridge, and leads past the National Trust sign and along a gravelled path up the beautiful river valley. Pass a gate and when the path splits keep right, to cross a gated footbridge, to the point you would have reached after crossing the stepping stones near the church.

The river is in a gorge at this point, and we turn left to walk upstream along the right side of the river. Climb away from the stream for a short distance, through a gate but continue walking upstream, in the midst of lush greenery, where occasional grassy patches are covered with colourful wild flowers. Behind a few fir trees on the right is a small tarn, in a quite idyllic setting.

Good views then open up looking towards Hardknott with rugged hills over to the left, as we proceed along a grassy track through gorse bushes. A few cattle and many sheep are grazing in the valley fields, and more sheet are dotted like daisies high up on the fells, where little white specks can be picked out on steep slopes and even on rocky crags.

Go through a gate and over a footbridge, and then through a narrow wood with some old trees, many with huge patches of lichen, and there may even be a few fungi if the summer has been wet (as in 1998). The track goes past Low Birker and then heads down to the stream again to reach Doctor Bridge **(3)**, a stone built pack horse bridge. Do not go over the bridge but turn right on the public bridleway to Penny Hill Farm, and walk through the farmyard, passing to the right of the farm. Keep straight ahead although the track bends slightly right beyond the farm, but is clearly signed with blue arrows.

Go through a gate and ignore the path turning off to the right. Keep straight on along a track, with trees and the river to our left, to reach a gate and stile, then walk along the edge of a wood – rich in bird life; look out for tree creepers. Cross another stream and pass a left turn **(4)** signposted to Wha House Bridge, but keep ahead following the sign to Hardknott.

The path narrows through bracken, and we bear slightly left to reach a footbridge and a small gate which leads us into a small wood. Follow the path near the wall on the left, with excellent views left up Brotherilkeld Valley, with open deciduous woodland with grassy floor and probably sheep, on our right. The view to the left opens out to reveal more peaks towards Bowfell and Scafell.

Leave the wood through a kissing gate, cross a stream and get into more bracken, and then through another kissing gate and descend slightly to the stone wall and small wood, which like so many of the small deciduous and mixed woods are rich in bird life including pied flycatchers. Notice the red telephone box on the "main" road down to the left as we just keep straight on, through two kissing gates and descend to the stream Hardknott Gill, a tributary of the Esk. Cross Jubilee Bridge and reach the road, at the foot of Hardknott Pass **(5)**.

We walk up the road, using the verge and taking short cuts through the grass on many of the zigzags, with the river to our right in a gorge lined with trees. As the road climbs it moves away from the stream, and every few metres the views back along Eskdale become even better, and in the distance on a clear day the sea and the Isle of Man will be visible. At the end of the stone wall on the left, notice the footpath sign going left – for later use.

Continue uphill, but soon take a diagonal path going up to the left, through some high level types of vegetation including sphagnum and bog cotton, to reach the wall of the fort, near the west gate and a small notice board, giving information about the structure of the wall.

After exploring the remnants of the fort, retrace steps from the west gate, back towards, but not as far as the road, to the wall and footpath sign noticed on the way up. Just a few metres along this wall, not far from the road, is a narrow pinch stile, and our path goes through here and steeply down a narrow path, with the road to our left. At the bottom of this slope is a wall and a small wood, and in the left corner of the field is a ladder stile. Head towards though not over this stile as it leads to the road and Jubilee Bridge, but instead, turn right to walk alongside the wall. Continue past the end of the wood, and straight ahead are good views up Brotherilkild valley, and when we reach a track at a T junction **(6)**, with Esk Falls signed right, turn left to walk through the gates and the farmyard. Once past the buildings of this 17th century farmhouse, turn sharp right along the riverside path, as far as the wooden footbridge – a memorial to Dick Marsh who died in the hills in August 1964 at the age of 38. Cross the bridge and then a stile to walk along the narrow permissive path heading straight towards Taw House (which is known to have been visited by Samuel Taylor Coleridge). This narrow path may be wet or overgrown, or both, and after two stiles and then another stile, we reach the farm. A footpath is signed right to Scafell, but we turn left into the farmyard, and then right-left, and along the stony track to head away from the buildings. Look out for the yellow flowers of bog asphodel which grows in the acid soils of some of the wetter areas.

Pass a lone small house, Birdhow, now a holiday cottage owned by the National Trust, and continue along the drive to pass the cattle grid and reach the end of the wall on the left (7). We can either go left down a grassy path through bracken to reach the road – or just continue along the track. The choice depends on whether you wish to walk along the road or not.

Either: turn left along the road and walk to the Whahouse Bridge over the River Esk, and a few metres past this is a public bridleway sign along the river. Follow the left bank of the river until the river begins to bend round to the right and here go straight ahead and follow the bridleway up into the woods. This leads to a T-junction of paths where we walked earlier (4). Turn right and retrace steps to Penny Hill Farm and Doctor Bridge. Go over the bridge and turn left to join the alternative route described below, walking down the right bank of the river.

Or: if continuing along the road, just follow the track until it ends and turn right along the road. This will lead past Eskdale Youth Hostel, and what will seem to be the even more impressive Woolpack Inn if you are in need of accommodation, food or drink. Just past the Woolpack on the left is the driveway to Pennyhill Farm offering self catering or bed and breakfast, and turn down this driveway to the bridge over the river, and join the alternative route (3). Do not cross this bridge, but turn right through a gate to walk between the river and a wall.

Both routes have merged as we continue alongside the river or just one field away from the river. Across the valley at the top of the very steep slope may be seen the white water of Birker Force. Keep ahead through bracken or grass and when the path splits go down to the left to reach the river at Gill Force bridge, seen on the outward journey. From here retrace steps along the gravelled path to the church and then the track back to Boot.

September

Windermere to Troutbeck

*A glorious walk into one of Lakeland's most beautiful and unspoilt
valleys, with visits to a remarkable old house in Troutbeck and the
National Park Centre at Brock Hole. Everchanging views of the
surrounding hills are an outstanding feature of this walk.*

Length: 11 miles with a short-cut option of 7½ miles

Time required: 6 hours (or 4 for the short cut)

Terrain: a few ascents but nothing which is very steep.

Map: O.S. 1:25,000 Outdoor Leisure number 7, The English Lakes South
Eastern Area.

Starting point: GR414987, on the A591 near Windermere station. Car
parking is available in Windermere.

Facilities: Trains and buses run to Windermere, which contains a choice
of pubs and cafes, as well as a Tourist Information Centre (015394
46499)

Weather

The month often has a fine settled spell and this year (1998) was no
exception. The early part of the month contained several very wet
days, with more than half an inch of rainfall on each of the 1st, 8th,
9th and 10th, followed by a week of sunshine and showers. Around
the time of the equinox, when the sun is directly overhead at the
equator, all parts of the world receive equal amounts of daylight. At
this time, from the 18th-25th, the Lake District enjoyed a very sunny
week, nearly coinciding with a well known spell of weather in the
period 13-17th, which records show to be one of the driest weeks of

the year – though not one of the spells recorded by Buchan. This spell of settled anticyclonic weather was particularly appreciated after a generally wet summer season. Overnight mists and dews occurred and small temperature inversions occurred, when the colder air rolled down to the bottom of the valleys but slightly warmer air remained a few hundred feet above. At this warmer layer, any smoke from bonfires or chimneys would spread out horizontally, as it would be unable to rise higher, through the warmer layer of air. Traditionally the month ends the summer and brings in the autumn, and September sees a noticeable shortening of the daylight hours, as mentioned in Maxwell Anderson's "September Song".

> And the days grow short,
> when you reach September.

The countryside

Nature too is affected by the shortening days, as the period of growth is slowing, and plants begin to shrivel and fade, though some flowers such as toadflax and harebells are still brightening the wayside. Fruits and berries will be increasing and may even be prolific (an indication of a suitable summer, not a forecast of a hard winter). The hedgerow harvests are a great help to birds and animals who begin to build up layers of fat to help through the winter or to help provide energy for migration. Many of the summer birds have gone, but house martins and swallows can still be seen, as well as a few warblers, and early in the month on this walk, there will still be redstarts and flycatchers. By the end of the month most of the summer visitors have gone and the resident birds may be gathering in flocks. Groups of tits will be touring in the woods on their search for food, and will be starting to include gardens in their circuits. Flocks of starlings are steadily growing in number, as they accumulate on wires or trees, and large groups of rooks and jackdaws can be seen in the evenings as they fly lazily to wherever they happen to be roosting. Ducks will be out in the lakes again, in showy colour in the case of the males, after their virtual disappearance act in August, whilst moulting. As the males reappear in full colour they may even begin to pair off. Squirrels will be active gathering food and burying any surplus for future use. It is unlikely that they remember exactly where it is buried, but general location may be known and the food is subsequently discovered in the winter, by the use of smell. Out on the hills gorse may be flowering, but bracken will be turning yellow and long tentacles of blackberries stretch across the paths. In the fields the hay has been made and cattle and sheep are to be seen everywhere.

Scots Pine, Troutbeck

Windermere

This famous town is the southern gateway into the Lake District though it is situated one mile away from its namesake lake, which, extending for 10½ miles is the longest lake in England. With rows of shops, hotels, pubs and cafes, it is a busy centre, and has bus links with much of the Lakes and has a railway station where the shuttle service to Oxenholme Junction provides frequent links to the main London to Glasgow line. The arrival of the railway in 1847 was a major factor in the growth of the town. The church of Windermere St Mary dates from 1848, but is a strange mixture of features, as additions and changes were made in the 1850s, 1860s and 1880s. There are 4 other churches in the town.

Troutbeck

Village, river and valley all have the same name. Early Norse settlers in the 9th and 10th centuries found the valley bottom too wet and wooded for settlements and so they built their farmhouses in a linear pattern on the drier and sunnier slopes, generally where there was a water supply. Many of the buildings in the elongated village are quite close to wells which can still be seen if you walk through the village. Early buildings were of wood and turf, but stone became the main building material by the 16th century. Most of the present day buildings are of stone and a few of the larger houses are impressive

A view into the Troutbeck Valley

Statesmen's Houses, built by the Yeomen farmers in the 16th century. In summer the village is very colourful, with well tended gardens, including the garden at Townend. Several houses now offer bed and breakfast, and many of the smaller houses are available for self-catering. Two pubs are located at the northern end of the village, and one of these, the Mortal Man was established in 1689, and has an interesting signboard painted by Julius Caesar Ibbetson, a local artist who lived in Troutbeck from 1801-1805. It is open all day. A well-known local rhyme comments about drinking habits:

Oh Mortal Man, thou liv'st on bread, How comes thy nose to be so red?
Thou silly ass that looks so pale, It is by drinking Birkett's Ale.

Townend

This Statesman's House was in the hands of the Browne family from 1626 until 1943 and is now managed by the National Trust. A stone farmhouse, it has mullioned windows and tall round chimneys and contains many items of furniture carved by members of the Browne family. The last of the males in this family was the George Browne who lived from 1834-1914 (there had been earlier George Brownes), and he was a collector and a woodcarver, and much of the furniture to be seen in the house today shows his work. At his death, Townend

Townend

was left to his surviving daughter who died in 1943, was accepted by the Treasury in 1945 to cover the Estate Duty and was transferred to the National Trust in 1947. The contents were also retained in the house, including furniture made especially to fit. The house is kept much has it would have been in former centuries. There is a delightful garden, and across the road is Townend Farm with its remarkable 17th century Bank barn. Bank barns are barns built on a slope and having the entrance to a cowshed on the lower side, with a ramp on the other side leading to the upper level, which would be used as a hayloft. Similar barns are found in Scandinavia as well as elsewhere in the Lake District. The house is open from 1st April to 1st November, Tuesdays to Fridays, and Sundays plus Bank Holiday Mondays, from 1pm-5pm, or dusk if earlier.

Jesus church

This small church stands by the main road, not up in the main part of the village of Troutbeck. The large east window is by Burne Jones, who was visited by his friends William Morris and Ford Maddox Brown, who came for a fishing holiday, but were persuaded to help with his work. The window contains a large amount of green, which is unusual, but he was a 'green' person. The church probably dates from the 15th century but was largely rebuilt in 1736, and changed in the 19th century too.

Brock Hole

The Lake District Visitor Centre is situated on the main A591 between Windermere and Ambleside, and is open daily from the beginning of April until the beginning of November, from 10am till 5.00pm, though the grounds and gardens are open all year. There is pay and display parking but free entry for walkers. The centre is in a mansion built last century for William Henry Gaddum, a Manchester business man. It provides information about many aspects of the National Park and numerous special events take place here. It has a lake shore in the grounds and a 45-minute cruise from Brock Hole to Waterhead is available from May to October.

The walk

Walk from the car park **(1)** through the town towards the main Kendal to Ambleside road, the A591. Cross over by the TIC and turn left for about 30 metres as far as the broad surfaced path signposted to Orrest Head (784 feet or 239 metres) with unrivalled views of the fells, as well as the lake. The path soon splits, with the left turn to Troutbeck (our return route), but we keep straight ahead and climbing, following white arrows to Orrest viewpoint. Though part of the path is shady beneath trees, occasional views soon begin to open up. Pass Elleray Wood cottage at the end of the surfaced track, but keep ahead on a stony track, and when the path splits take the right fork alongside the wall. Climb steeply up beneath tall trees, and then at the T-junction turn right, between a wall and a wire fence. Seats along this section provide a resting point if required, with good views – but there are better views to come. Turn left at an iron kissing gate, where there is a memorial stone to Arthur Henry Haywood of Elleray, as a mark of gratitude to his widow and daughter who dedicated Orrest Head to the use of the public. Climb the stone staircase to the summit, where there are plenty of seats, extensive all round views and a toposcope pointing out a few of the features visible on a clear day – including Coniston Old Man, Sca Fell Pike, Harrison Stickle.

There is a choice of path down the grassy slopes, but head towards the white farm to the north, and descend to a wall, which is unseen at first, but soon comes into sight. Find the stone stile, near an iron gate, and follow the path more or less straight ahead, with a stone wall a few metres to the left. Gradually descend through a large field, with scattered hawthorn probably rich in berries, and the white farm seen from the top is now slightly to the left. At the end of the field is a high stone stile, near an iron gate which leads on to the narrow road and we turn right along the road **(2)**. Just before reaching the house on the left (Near Orrest), at the sign to Far Orrest go left over a stone stile, and walk by the wall along the field margin, passing the side of the buildings, which include a bank barn.

Go through a wooden kissing gate, cross another small field, to a kissing gate, a small wood and then a stone stile. Cross the next field to a stone stile on the corner of the wall, and continue along the right side of the next field, to a tall wooden ladder stile. At the end of the

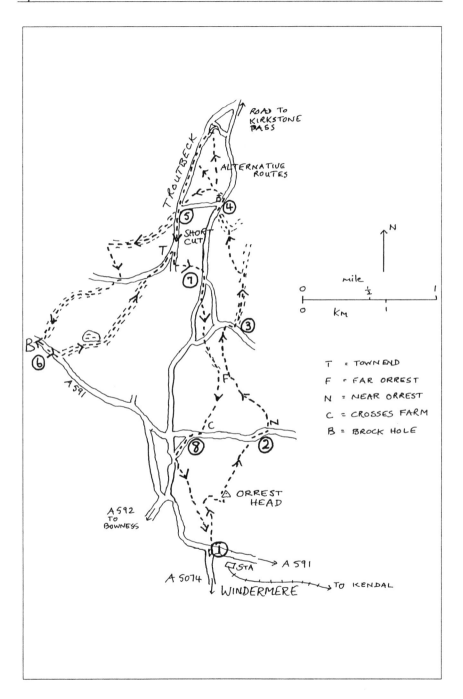

ROAD TO
KIRKSTONE
PASS

TROUTBECK

ALTERNATIVE
ROUTES

⑤
B
④

SHORT
CUT

T

⑦

⑥ B

A 591

⑤

③

F

F

N

C

⑧

②

ORREST
HEAD

A 592
TO
BOWNESS

①

STA   → A 591

A 5074

↓ WINDERMERE   → TO KENDAL

N

mile
0   ½   1
0   KM

T = TOWN END
F = FAR ORREST
N = NEAR ORREST
C = CROSSES FARM
B = BROCK HOLE

next meadow is another ladder stile, and after the next field we reach a small wooden kissing gate alongside a larger wooden gate. The sign to Troutbeck and Garburn points us the 10 metres to another small kissing gate, after which we turn left, and walk past the farm buildings and then left again through a small kissing gate, after which we turn right. Walk along the green track between stone walls, and another view of Windermere, which keeps appearing throughout this walk. Pass a line of fir trees on the left, and then an area of open fell to the right, and keep straight ahead through a gap in the wall, along the track across the grassy slope, with magnificent views now to be seen up the Troutbeck valley, with the linear village of Troutbeck stretching along the opposite valley side.

At the end of the field go through the rather narrow kissing gate on to a road **(3)** and turn right for just over 100 metres and then turn left. This is Longmire Road, a narrow road to Kentmere and Garburn Pass. Ascend slightly, and after reaching the wood on the right, the surfaced road becomes a stony track, and once past the end of the wood, look for our turning to the left, off the track, to go over a stone stile and descend alongside the small stream. Just before reaching a wall and the buildings of Longmire, turn right, for a fairly level stretch alongside a row of trees, which include some beech. At the end of the field go over a ladder stile, and diagonally down across the next field where thistles and buttercups might be in flower, to a stone stile by a wooden gate, and straight on, with a wall to our left. The views ahead up the right side of Troutbeck valley, show peak after peak, up towards Ill Bell and High Street. At the next stone stile and gate, reach a stony track, and turn left to go steeply downhill, passing the The Howe, a farm complex, with dovecote, and walk through a small wood alongside a tumbling stream, to the road, A592 **(4)**.

Turn right and take the footpath alongside the road, cross the footbridge over the Trout Beck, cross the narrow side road and visit the Jesus church, with its large clock dated 1887. A track along the right side of the church leads away from the main road up towards the village. The first turn off the track is a path to the right, over a stile by the wooden gate, and this will lead you to the northern end of the village near The Mortal Man, if you wish to visit a pub, and then walk through the length of the village. If not, keep straight ahead and just beyond the bridge over the small stream there is another right turn which leads to the middle of the village, but walk straight ahead for the shortest route through Troutbeck. This leads through the gate, and on up to High Fold Farm, B and B, to reach the main village street, where we turn left to pass the top of the narrow road coming up from the A592, and then the Post Office (may have cups of tea or coffee if it is open), situated in the old Village Institute **(5)**.

Here is the point of decision. The main route forks right off the road on the stony track, but the alternative keeps straight along the road for the short cut

Short cut

For a walk of 7½ miles rather than 11 miles, keep straight ahead along the road, which divides outside Townend, and if you wish to visit this remarkable old Statesman's House, now is the time, if it is open. For the onward route, fork left at this road junction, and begin to walk downhill, passing the magnificent old Bank barn with gallery on the left, and then Townend Farm. All the buildings in the village are of interest, and at Townsfoot House, with its line of stones protruding at each floor level, a bridleway comes from the right, and another goes to the left, which is where we turn. This leads steeply down to the Trout Beck, across two footbridges via an island in mid stream, through a gate, and steeply up a field to reach another of those narrow kissing gates and out on to the pavement. Walk alongside the main road **(7)** for 350m., and then go left diagonally up a grassy field, passing a large conifer, and walking along a terrace, to reach Annie's Seat beneath a large beech tree, just before the group of buildings. Go over a stile and through the farmyard, along the drive to a narrow road, and straight across and ahead along the driveway signposted to Far Orrest Farm. We follow this as it passes above and to the left of the large buildings of Holehird, with the small lake.

Go into the middle of the collection of buildings at Far Orrest, and turn right following the signpost to Windermere via Crosses. Once beyond the farmyard and all the buildings go on to a track crossing the middle of a field to a gate, alongside which is a tall ladder stile. The path and track continue across the next field and we bend left just before a gap in the wall, to stay alongside the wall, and reach a gate and a stone stile. Continue straight ahead across two fields, to a driveway and past the buildings out on to a narrow road **(8)**. The main buildings of Crosses are just to our left, but we turn right along the road, soon to descend steeply, through a wood, and on the right can be seen part of St Anne's School. At the bottom of the hill, at the A592, turn left through a large iron gate, following the signpost to Orrest Head.

After about 100 metres the path splits and we fork right (straight ahead really) along the gravel path, across the driveway and towards the woods. Go through an iron gate, cross a footbridge and follow the clear path through the woods. Just keep straight ahead until reaching a surfaced driveway which crosses our path, and to the left is the entrance gate to Elleray Bank. Cross this drive and keep straight on along the narrow path which now has an open meadow to the right. Pass to the left of North's Point and soon we are joined by a path from Orrest Head which comes in from the left, and we keep straight on until we reach the surfaced path where we began our walk up to Orrest Head. Turn right down to the main road, where we cross over to the Tourist Information Centre and back into Windermere. Back in the different world of Windermere, with traffic and people.

Main route

Fork right off the road, on the stony track. Notice the old sign on the south wall of the P.O. – Troutbeck Village Institute 1869 – as we set off along Robin Lane, following the old signpost pointing to Ambleside and Jenkin Crag. Walk along this bridleway, a stony track which takes us past Number One, Robin Lane, called Shepherd's cottage, now a holiday cottage with a lovely garden. Wild flowers line this track, including rose bay willow herb and blackberries, the latter having some ripe berries as well as red berries and white flowers. Birds around here include crows, jackdaws, and buzzards. We soon pass a seat, situated where a track goes down to the left, and also where the view to Windermere is magnificent.

At a stone stile on the right, there is a short path up to the tall cairn, from where the views are excellent. Just a few yards beyond this stile is a grassy track where we turn left, for only 20 metres before going left again, over a stile by a wooden gate, and walk on the grassy path going downhill, with a small stream to our left. Flowers along this path include sorrel, thistles, tormentil, and meadow sweet on the edge of the stream. Pass the National Trust sign for Martin's Wood, then go over a stile and on downhill between two walls, with a wood to our right. We descend quite steeply to a narrow road, where we turn right for 20 metres and then go left between buildings of Castle Syke Farm.

Follow this stony bridleway as it goes downhill between walls and to a gate by a stile. Keep straight ahead, passing a small wood on the right, and join a major track, to descend steeply and pass to the left of Wood Farm buildings. Once past the buildings, go right, off the drive and follow the Footpath and Bridleway sign, leading through the trees, across a narrow stream, through a gate and on to a track between walls. This continues along the margin of the wood to our right – probably full of bird noises in spring and summer, though now fairly quiet with only a robin, wren and nuthatch to be heard singing, though a few tits, greater spotted woodpeckers, and jays might be heard calling. Beech mast lines the path in several locations. Ignore the path going off to the right, as we keep straight ahead, with a wall on the left. Descend steeply to join a driveway by Merewood Lodge, a Peter Chadwick Training Centre, and arrive at the main road (6).

Our onward route is to the left, but first turn right to visit Brock Hole, the National Park Centre, where there are toilets, refreshments, picnic area, information and displays, with free entry for pedestrians. After a visit to Brock Hole, return to the main road and turn right for 250 yards, passing the end of Mirk Lane on the left, opposite St Andrews Ecclerigg on the right. Then, where the main road bends right, cross over to go left, not at the first driveway which leads to a large house, but a few yards further at the public Bridleway called Wain Lane, which is an old road formerly linking Windermere and Troutbeck.

Follow this track, and soon cross a small stream over a stone slab footbridge, and pass a few prolific blackberry bushes. The lane bends to the right, and on the left behind the stone wall is a man-made lake created early this century. Herons and ducks may be seen on here, and early in the month swallows and house martins may be flying low over the water. Deer are often to be seen nearby. Near the end of the lake, the lane bends left and begins to climb, giving good views over the lake and revealing a house at the far end. Alongside this lane, colour is provided by the red berries on the hawthorn and rowan, and the first leaves on horse chestnut and sycamore turning to yellow and brown. Climbing up the slope we pass a bank barn on the right, with its two stories and the ramp to the upper level being clearly seen. There are other barns in nearby fields, and as we climb higher the lane becomes sunken, with overhanging trees, and tree roots at head height. The track levels off and at the minor road turn right, to walk round to the first houses of Troutbeck, then the car park for Townend and the road junction alongside which the house Townend is located. Here we turn sharp right on the B class road to Windermere, and follow the instructions given in the Short cut section above.

October

Coniston

From Coniston with its famous lake, this walk takes in woodland and meadow on its way to Tarn Hows, thought by many to be the most attractive spot in the Lake District. The return is downhill all the way through the woods, and then an extension walk climbs up from the other side of the village to the devastated landscape of the old copper mines.

Length: 5½ miles with an extra 1½ to walk round the lake at Tarn Hows. The extension to the Coppermine area will add about 3½ miles, to give a total of 10½.

Time required: 3-4 hours for Tarn Hows and a further 2 hours for the copper mines.

Terrain: gentle climbing to Tarn Hows, but there is a steeper climb to the copper mines. Paths are clear, but can often be muddy.

Maps: O.S. 1:25,000 Outdoor Leisure maps 6 and 7, the South West and the South East Lake District.

Starting point: the car park in Coniston (GR304975), reached along the A593 from Ambleside. Another car park is located at the old railway station.

Facilities: Nearest station is at Windermere, but regular buses go through Coniston. Nearest town is Ambleside and there is a Tourist Information Centre in Coniston (015394 41533) Refreshments – good choice in Coniston.

Weather

The middle month of autumn generally gives a taste of all seasons, with sun, rain, wind and occasional frosts. In the Lakes the daily maxima temperatures were mostly about 15°, though down to 10° for most of the last week. Occasional sunny days occurred but there was some rain on most days, generally showery with sunny periods and often very clear air giving good views. However, more than 1 inch fell on each of the 13th, 16th, 27th and 2.3 inches was recorded at Keswick on the 21st. Rainfall was brought by a series of Atlantic depressions which were very deep and associated with winds up to 80 mph as well as heavy rain. The worst of the rain and floods occurred in the Midlands, but most of the country, including the Lake District had a wetter than average month.

Two old sayings about the weather of the month are:

> *A thunderstorm in October is a sign of a long cold winter;*

and

> *As the weather in October so it will be next March.*

These must have been true in one year, or these sayings would not have originated, but they are unlikely to be true every year. There is no direct connection between the weather of these different months, and October's weather will be totally unrelated to conditions in December or March.

The countryside

One outstanding feature of this autumnal month is the changing colour of the leaves. Even though the strong winds were blowing leaves, and branches, off the trees early in the month, the wet weather enabled leaves to hang around right through the month – enhancing the already glorious scenery in the Coniston landscape. Overlooking the small town and lake is the prominent Coniston Old Man, also known as Kanchenjunga to Arthur Ransome's readers. The green landscape of the hills is broken on lower Coniston Old Man by the remnants of mining and quarrying, as important to the local economy as tourism is nowadays, and a fascinating place to visit. The hills have their everpresent crows and ravens, and the smaller birds such as pipits and skylarks are still in the hills until driven down into the valleys by colder weather. Peregrines, sparrowhawks and kestrels are predators which may be seen as they go about their business of hunting their daily meal, but they have much less work to do now that they are not also feeding their young. Kestrels are most easily seen because their method of hunting is to float as though suspended on a string, whilst searching for a vole or a beetle. The other two are less easily seen as their hunting style is different. Winter visitor birds are beginning to arrive, with fieldfares and redwings in the woods and on the farmland, and more ducks and sawbills settling in on the lakes. Mallard and teal breed here, but numbers are swollen by many arrivals in autumn.

The woodlands not only have all shades of leaves from green through yellows to brown, but the colours of numerous fungi can also be spotted if you look carefully whilst walking in any woodland.

Harebell

Coniston

This small village has been closely linked with mining and quarrying in the past, but now mainly provides amenities for the large numbers of visitors who come each year. Surrounded by impressive fells and miles of walking, Coniston is also noted for its famous lake. The stone church of St Andrew was restored in 1891 and contains few relics of former buildings. In the churchyard is the John Ruskin Memorial, an impressive carved Cross, the work of W.G. Collingwood. Several of Ruskin's relatives are also buried here. Collingwood, who also designed the War Memorial near the South Porch, is buried close by, beneath a very modest stone. There is a small Ruskin Museum in Coniston, but a much bigger exhibition in Brantwood overlooking the lake where he lived for 28 years (1872-1900) – see the December walk. Coniston Hall, just south of the village was the home of the Fleming family from 1250 onwards, for about 500 years. The present building with its distinctive chimney was 17th century, and was abandoned in the 18th century. It later became a farmhouse and is now owned by the National Trust.

Coniston Water

Over 5 miles long, this lake is famous for its boating and fishing. Donald Campbell died here in his attempt to break the world water speed record in 1967. The lake is lined with trees and contains many small bays and stony beaches. Regular boat services run from Coniston Quay in the two launches, *ML Ruskin* and *ML Ransome*. There is also the famous steam yacht *Gondola*, first launched in 1859. This was built to carry tourists, and was restored to its original specifications in 1980. The *Gondola* runs its scheduled steam boat service from Coniston Pier to Park-a-Moor and Brantwood, from 1st April until 1st November. Brantwood overlooks the lake from the eastern side. Another famous name associated with Coniston is Arthur Ransome. Swallows and Amazons, perhaps his most famous title was based on a mixture of Coniston and Windermere. Peel Island (National Trust) on Coniston was the idea for the Secret Harbour of Wild Cat Island, and on the east side of Coniston is Bank Ground Farm, the basis of Holly Howe where Swallows stayed for the holidays.

The Coniston launch

Tarn Hows

There were originally three small hollows in this area, surrounded by farmland where sheep were reared, and farmers and weavers lived in a community called Tarn Hows. Quarrying for limestone and production of wood for charcoal were other activities. The land was owned by Monk Coniston Hall which was probably built by the monks of Furness Abbey in the 13th century. The Monk Coniston Estate was bought by James Marshall in 1835, and he enlarged it from 670 to over 4000 acres, and one of his many changes in the area was to dam Tom Gill. The dam is only 33 ft long and 9 ft high, but it transformed the previous three small tarns into the present day lake. The stream was used as a source of water power for saw milling down in the valley. He also planted many trees and shrubs, including rhododendron and rowan. The estate was bought by Mrs. Heelis in 1929, who subsequently sold part of it to the National Trust and bequeathed the rest in her will. Because of its varied plant and animal life it was designated a Site of Special Scientific Interest in 1965, and among its many attractions are pond plants, dragonflies, golden eye ducks, goosander and mergansers, and in the nearby woods are several sparrow hawks. Black-headed gulls are likely to be scavenging from picnickers.

Tarn Hows cottage in its snug location

Copper mining

Development of copper mining began in the 16th century when
Daniel Hochstetter, the German mining engineer, found rich lodes
of copper in the area. The German miners who were already working
near Keswick came to extract copper, which was sent to Keswick for
smelting. Galleries and shafts are numerous in the valley and spoil
heaps are still evident. Higher up the valley than the coppermines
are the spoil heaps and remnants of slate quarrying which was important here for centuries. Rocks and minerals were carried by packhorse, sled or cart down to the lake, and then by boat to the southern
end of the lake. From there they went by road to the port of
Greenodd. After 1859 the ore went by train. The houses in the valley, now holiday cottages, were built for the miners. The peak period
for the mining was in the middle of the 19th century, when 400 people were employed, but decline was rapid after 1875, because of
cheaper ore from overseas. The Copper mines get a mention in Arthur Ransome's "Pigeon Post".

The Walk

From the car park **(1)** near the centre of Coniston, walk out to the
main road, crossing the small green next to the car park where there
is a public seat. Here is the memorial to Donald Campbell who died
on Coniston Water on January 4th 1967, and also a memorial to Leo
Villa O.B.E. the chief mechanic to Campbell who died in 1979.

Cross over from the car park and turn right, along Tilberthwaite
Avenue, the road towards Tarn Hows and Hawkshead, and just before reaching the bridge over the river, turn left along the narrow
road signposted to Ambleside. The stream is on our right, and we
pass the Coniston football pitch, before turning right over a stone
bridge, and immediately go left over a stone stile and through a
wooden kissing gate, on to the left margin of a field. The clear path
goes across the field and then alongside a wall and a fence as we begin to climb. Coniston Water will be visible over to the right, with
the white buildings of Brantwood further to the right, on the slope at
the foot of the woodland.

At the end of the field go through a kissing gate and pass to the left
of an old ruin, continuing to climb. Go through a gate and straight on

up the next field, and then through a patch of gorse to a stile, wooden kissing gate and into the woods. Walk through the woods (Guards Wood) to a gate and then on across a grassy field, and near the end of the field bear slightly left to go through a gap in the wall and on to a stile and a gate, with a signpost. Coniston is back the way we have come, left is Low Yewdale and Tarn Hows, and right is Boon Crag.

We turn left along the stony track and just before the stone bridge (2) over the beck, turn right over a stile following the signpost to Tarn Hows. Walk along the margin of the field with the stream to our left and, at the end of the field, go over the stile on to the narrow path into the trees. The Yewdale Beck is just to the left, with a flat valley floor, and the dramatic crags of Yewdale Fells beyond. Our path begins to climb up and away from the river, through quite open woodland, which is mainly deciduous and very colourful at this time of year. Cross a small footbridge and then continue to climb. Reach a deer fence and a high level gate for walkers. Do not go through here but walk alongside the fence, over a footbridge and climb up to a track at a large gate and another of the high level small gates on a stile. Turn left along the track and reach the edge of the wood, with fine views over the wall, looking down to High Yewdale. Bird noises around here may be the mewing of buzzards overhead, or the gronk, gronk of ravens, with little sissing noises of the tits and goldcrests in the woods. The path leads on through two gates to reach the front of the delightful Tarn Hows Cottage in its rather isolated location. Turn right through the next gate to walk along the driveway as it leads out to a narrow road (3).

Just before reaching this road, turn left to go steeply down a gravelled bridleway, and follow this for about a quarter mile, until the road on the valley floor comes into sight more than 100 metres ahead. Turn right through a wooden gate, where two tracks may be noticed but take the clearer right fork, which bends right, round the slope and is situated between the old remnants of an ancient and tumbledown wall. The track leads across a field and bends right towards an old ruined farmhouse, but turns sharp left to zigzag up the slope, just before reaching the ruins. As we climb there is a wall on our left, and we head up towards a wood. The grassy track bends right alongside the wall and the wood, and we reach a large wooden gate where we turn left. Go through here and follow the track as it climbs steeply up through bracken and then trees to the top of the

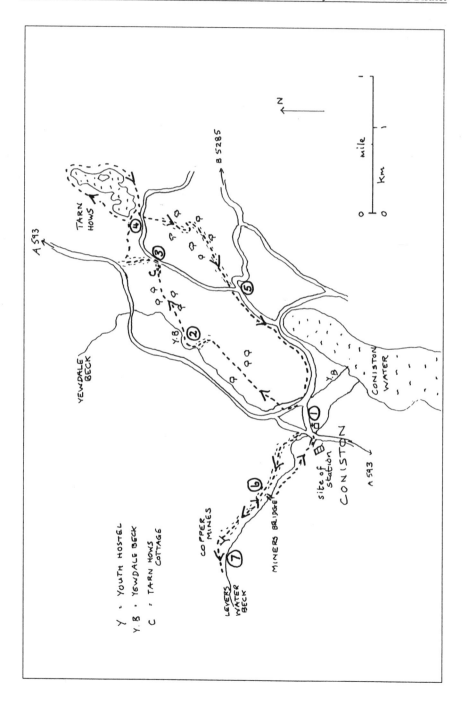

slope, when we catch our first glimpse of Tarn Hows **(4)**. Descend to this beautiful spot – and have a picnic – perhaps. To our left is the lake and to our right is the road, and a National Trust car park, which is unlikely to be empty – whatever day or time you arrive.

The onward walk is to the right of the lake, alongside the car park, but the circuit of the lake is highly recommended, with a clear path to follow and everchanging views to the surrounding hills.

On we go, following the clear and broad path to the left of the car park, which descends through the woods, crosses a small stream, which is then on our left. Reach a sharp left bend quickly followed by a sharp right bend, as we cross over the stream and are joined by a track coming in from the left. Continue down the valley to reach a junction of paths where left is signed to Hollin Bank and Wharton Tarn, but we go right towards Boon Crag and Coniston. The stream is now to our right, as we pass a few old tall conifers, with very soft bark in which a fern may be seen growing. A carpet of leaves lines the path here and elsewhere, at this time of year. We cross the stream which is then in a deep ravine to our left, with numerous ferns beneath the trees, some of which are tall and old specimens. The path soon emerges at a narrow road, with a slightly larger road a few yards to the left **(5)**.

Cross straight over the narrow road, through a wooden gate and follow the path along the left side of the stream. We emerge on to the major road (B5285) just before Boon Crag, and Monk Coniston Hall (National Trust- now let to the Holiday Fellowship) is across on the left of the road. There is a bridleway leading right between the buildings of Boon Crag, but we can stay on the roadside, to follow the path between hedges, and off the road. This leads down towards the lake, and if you have good long vision you might just see windmills on the skyline several miles to the south of the lake. The road bends right, and leads us back to the village over the Yewdale Bridge and past the road to the right where we started the walk.

Extension

If time and energy remain, a fascinating walk to the old copper mines will lead you steeply up in the direction of Coniston Old Man. From near the church **(1)** and the centre of the village with all its pubs, hotels and cafes, walk along the narrow road to the right of the

Black Bull and go up this road passing the Ruskin Museum. Church Beck is in the trees to the left of the road, and the hedge on the right contains the distinctive white berries of the snowberry, a shrub imported from North America early last century. The surfaced road ends at the large house, Holywath, which was the residence of John Barratt in the 19th century. He was one of those who made a fortune from the copper mines further up the valley.

The road becomes a stony track as we pass the signpost to the Coppermines. Copper used to be brought down this track. Go on beyond the cattle grid and out on to the open fell, though with a stone wall on our left. We walk on up alongside the deep but narrow gorge containing Church Beck, and down in the shelter of this gorge are numerous trees, with dramatic rocky pools and waterfalls. Keep straight on past the Miner's Bridge **(6)**, which is the route of our return walk, and as the steady climb ends and we reach a more open and level area, the remnants of the mines come into sight. Old mines and mine debris can be seen straight ahead and up to the right as we approach the old buildings. The row of holiday cottages to the right is called Irish Row, after the origin of many of the labourers who came here to work in the mines.

As we approach the buildings, we see the Youth Hostel **(7)** on the left, in the middle is the Miners Cottage now the property of the Barrow Mountaineering and Ski Club, and on the right are a group of what are now holiday cottages. The Youth Hostel was the mine office, and the The Miners Cottage was erected in the mid 1820s as a residence for the Mine Captain, and part of the basement was a stable for horses. Notice the silver birch and box trees by the door.

There is a useful information board which explains the purposes of some of the buildings whose remains can just be seen beyond the Miners Cottage. Note and beware, that the old mines are very interesting, but are potentially very dangerous!

It is possible to walk on further to see more of the old mine area, but for just a short extension, go along the track to the left of the Youth Hostel and continue for a few hundred metres. This will lead past a building in the trees on the right, which was the gunpowder store, and as the track climbs further note the mini wood of juniper trees in the small valley to the left. Ahead can be seen the large quarry on the slopes of the Old Man, but perhaps now is the time to turn back and retrace steps along the main track down the valley.

On the descent there may be good views across the lake to Brantwood and Grizedale forest on the far slope, before we turn right over Miner's Bridge **(6)**, built when a branch line of the railway reached Coniston in 1859. Once over the bridge turn left along a rocky path, with a lovely gorge down to the left, full of autumnal colour. Go through the small wooden gate by a larger gate and keep straight on, between the walls. I hope you will be as lucky as I was on my last walk down this path as I saw a red squirrel in the woods to the left. It skilfully crossed the stream, using tree branches as a bridge.

As we cross a tributary stream, notice the building up to the right, now a workshop but formerly the site of the copper store at the end of the railway line which came across the fine stone bridge. Walk on through the middle of a field, still on a stony track, and go through a gate and the farmyard of Dixon Ground Farm. Turn right along the narrow road and at the T junction, the Sun Inn is on the left, and the centre of Coniston is down to the left. Before turning left, go right for a few metres up the hill to visit the old railway station, now the site of an Industrial Estate and a car park, though the railway platform can still be seen. The railway opened on 18th June 1859, mainly for the ore but also used for passengers. The station was enlarged in 1888 and a new tearoom added in 1905. Coal, timber and slate were carried after the decline of copper. The line was closed to passengers on 15th September 1958 and to goods traffic on 30th April 1962.

The Sun serves excellent food as well as the local Bluebird bitter. The beer is named after Donald Campbell's boat, and on the walls are many memories of his attempts on the World Speed Record, which was planned from this hotel. For one reason or another, The Sun is well worth a visit, before going on downhill, to the centre of the village.

November

Borrowdale

This short walk explores the imposing valley of Borrowdale, and gives wonderful views both to the main mass of the Lake district hills as well as north over Derwent Water.

Length: 6½ miles with a short-cut option of 5 miles.

Time required: 3-4 hours or an hour less for the shorter route.

Terrain: fairly gentle except for the steep climb up Castle Crag. Many of the paths are almost certain to be muddy.

Map: O.S. 1:25,000 Outdoor Leisure map number 4, The English Lakes, North Western area.

Starting point: at GR253168, and is reached along the B5289 from Keswick to Rosthwaite and Honister.

Facilities: Keswick is easily reached by bus, and occasional buses run along Borrowdale. Keswick is the nearest town and the location of a Tourist Information Centre (017687 72645)

Weather

This is the final month of autumn and can show spells of autumnal as well as occasionally winter weather. Usually a chilly spell will occur as a variation from milder weather, and this year (1998) frost, clear cold northerlies, snow, sunshine, mild weather, gale force winds were all experienced within a few days of each other, early in the month. One of the depressions contained the weakened remnants of the massive hurricane Mitch, which had devastated huge areas of the Caribbean two weeks earlier. Some rain fell on most days but as so often happens there were remarkable differences within a few miles, for instance a range from 0.06 inches at one weather station to 0.56 at another within 20 miles of each other. Even these small Cumbrian hills have considerable influence on the local weather. 1998 experienced a mild month, with several lovely sunny days, and the average daily maxima reached double figures, slightly warmer than the long-term average of 9-10°C.

The 11th of the month, St Martin's Day, was a mild day reaching a maximum of 10°C and the first cold spell occurred a week later. The old saying:

Ice before Martinmas enough to bear a duck
The rest of the winter is sure to be a muck.

Though this old saying suggesting that an early freeze-up will be the prelude to a mild winter has occasionally been true, this is not a reliable piece of weather lore. However a cold spell in November can often produce some wonderful views of mist over the lakes, much loved by both photographers and artists.

Looking over Seatoller into the Seathwaite valley

The countryside

This is often one of the wettest months of the year, and Borrowdale is noted for being the wettest place in England. But rain does not deter visitors to the Lake District, and it contributes to the tumbling streams, dramatic waterfalls and picturesque lakes, as well as creating the lovely lush green scenery. Thomas Hood's famous poem about November should not deter visitors either, as every year sees glorious exceptions to his gloom and doom:

> *No shade, no shine, no butterflies, no bees*
> *No fruit, no flowers, no leaves, no birds*
> *November.*

Sara Coleridge who knew the Lake District well, wrote an apt description of some days of this month with her famous lines:

> *Dull November brings the blast*
> *Then the leaves are falling fast.*

There are still a few leaves on the trees early in the month, and even after they have fallen, the yellow and brown leaves can be seen in piles in hedge bottoms or against the foot of stone walls, or crunching underfoot on the footpaths. Hedgerows which may have been cut or shorn will look very bare, but the uncut will contain a variety of red berries (holly and rowan), a few white berries, and in several places on this walk are the red of deadly nightshade. Alder trees in the marshy areas near the River Derwent have their small cones as well as catkins. The bracken is brown, though it can look golden if the sun shines on it. The larch trees, which are numerous in this valley, really can look golden early in the month, before they shed all their needles. Bird life is still all around though the summer visitors have gone, to be replaced by flocks of fieldfares. Chacking flocks of jackdaws and family groups of crows will be seen and heard on the lower fells, with the tits, goldcrests and robins in the woods. Pipits might still be seen on the fells though they descend into the valleys during the winter, whilst the ubiquitous wren is likely to be encountered at any height, making an extremely loud noise for such a small bird. Sheep, including some of the famous Herdwick, may still be on the lower fells or else down in the valley.

Borrowdale

This deep steep sided glacial valley is a very popular attraction for visitors, and thousands of walkers, climbers and campers come here each year. In the past the valley has been the home of quarrymen, charcoal burners, bobbin makers as well as farmers. There are still farmers but the main source of income now is tourism. The hamlet of Grange is one of the small settlements in this valley, and contains the small dale church of Holy Trinity, with its churchyard surrounded by thin slabs of local rock. It was built in 1860 and is reached by crossing the two arched bridge over the Derwent which uses a grassy island in the middle of the river. The name Borrowdale is derived from the Old Norse words meaning a valley with a fort (on Castle Crag). Other Old Norse names can be found at Rosthwaite, a clearing with heaps of stones; Seathwaite, a clearing amid the sedge; and Seatoller, a sheiling by the alder tree.

Holy Trinity, Grange-in-Borrowdale

Castle Crag

This dramatic hill does not quite reach a height of 1000ft (305m) yet dominates this part of the valley and provides spectacular views. Wainwright considered the square mile containing Castle Crag and the Jaws of Borrowdale to be the finest in the Lake District. Slight remnants of an Iron Age camp can be seen on Castle Crag, though the top has mostly been removed by quarrying. The quarry scars are mostly concealed by trees when seen from a distance, but keep to the path as you climb the crag, and keep away from the large quarry hole near the top. Castle Crag was given to the National Trust in 1920 by Sir William Hamer and his family in memory of their son John and the men of Borrowdale killed in World War I. There is a war memorial on the summit. In 1939 Lady Hamer gave 46 acres (18.6 ha.) of the lower slopes of Castle Crag as a memorial to Sir William.

Herdwick sheep

These hardy animals which may have been encountered on several of the twelve walks in this book, have been farmed for nearly 1000 years, and were certainly important to Monastic farming communities in the 12th century. The National Trust own 25,000 Herdwick, which they lease to their tenant farmers. There is a Herdwick Breeders Association, and although larger than a few years ago, the membership only accounts for about 50,000 of the 1.5 million sheep in Cumbria. The Herdwick may have originated from Scandinavia but another possibility is that they originated from some Spanish sheep shipwrecked off the coast at the time of the Spanish Armada. They are recognised by their white face, and the lambs are black though become greyer with age. The males are mostly slaughtered whilst young, but the ewes are polled, and may survive 20 years and produce up to 30 lambs. They are able to survive most weathers, and are particularly good at heafing, staying in their own territory and do not really need fencing in. They have been known to find their own way back to their home fell, if taken away to another fellside location. Beatrix Potter was a major supporter of the Herdwick and was contributory to the survival of the breed.

The Walk

The Bowder Stone National Trust car park **(1)** is in an old quarry just beyond Grange village, and a notice says 600 yards to the Bowder Stone – we will walk more than 6 miles before we get there however. As you walk down to the road, look at the valley wall opposite, with rugged rocks extending to the left, but a smoother slope to the right. This is the junction of the Borrowdale Volcanic rocks to the left, and the softer Skiddaw slates to the right.

Turn left over the stone bridge, and note at the far end on the right, the bridge is built on a large smoothed rock, smoothed by ice during the last advance of The Ice Age. There is also a smoothed rock on the left of the bridge, behind the house and the Public toilets. Walk into Grange and notice the building stones – different types because of the variety in local rocks. Grange Bridge Cottage is on the left, with a *roche moutonnée* between it and the river, which can be clearly seen from outside the Gents. Pass the Tea Shop on the left and then our onward route is to the left just before reaching the church on the right-hand side. This lovely little church is well worth a visit – notice the stone slab wall round the churchyard.

Turn left along the stony track **(2)**, which is a Public Bridleway towards Honister, Rosthwaite and Seatoller. Notice the geological

The Bowder Stone

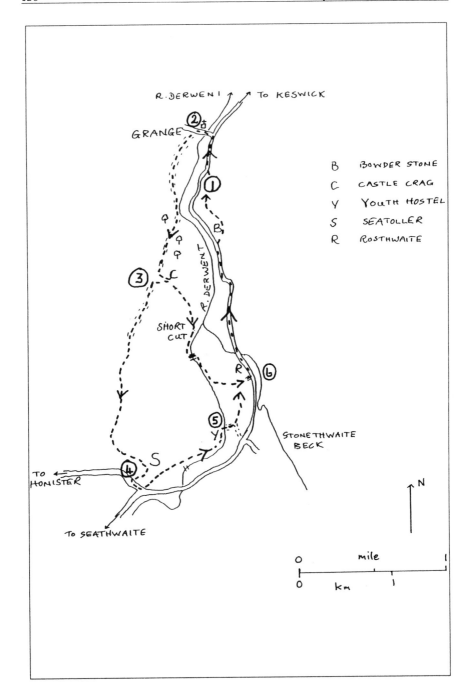

R. DERWENT → → TO KESWICK

GRANGE

B   BOWDER STONE
C   CASTLE CRAG
Y   YOUTH HOSTEL
S   SEATOLLER
R   ROSTHWAITE

R. DERWENT

B

C

SHORT CUT

R

STONETHWAITE BECK

S

TO HONISTER ←

TO SEATHWAITE

↑ N

0   mile   1
0   km   1

boundary up to the right. When the track splits, the surfaced lane goes straight ahead, but we turn left, passing a field on the left used as a camp site, with the wooded rocky hill of Holmcrag Hill (National Trust) beyond it – a fragment of harder rock which survived the erosive efforts of the ice. Then pass another camp site on the right, and our track comes quite close to the River Derwent for a few metres before going over a wooden footbridge and uphill into the woods, to reach an old quarry. Our path goes on to the left, with a stream down to the left, and we reach, but do not cross, a wooden sleeper footbridge. At this point we are joined by an alternative path coming up from the riverside, and keep straight on along a stony track. This track is the old pack horse route from the Rigghead Quarries. We climb steadily along a very stony track, with Broadslack Gill just to our left.

The rough stony track is still ascending through trees, but we reach a gate, beyond which is the open fell on the right, though with woods still on our left. The very steep slope to the right is littered with huge boulders which gradually (or, suddenly, but not very often) move down the slope and, in time, are broken up by frost shattering. The steep wooded slope to the left is Castle Crag.

Cross over the beck on several large stone slabs, and although our route continues straight ahead, we must make a detour **(3)** to the left for the fabulous views from the top of Castle Crag. Turn left along a clear path climbing quite steeply up to a stone stile and then a wooden ladder stile. Go on, over the wire fence which marks the bottom of the old quarries and follow the path as it meanders steeply up through the piles of rock debris. You may notice a stile over the wall to the right, for future reference.

Reach a flat area, where there are wonderful views up valley, over Rosthwaite village and straight up the Stonethwaite branch of Borrowdale. But there is even better to come, as a continuation up the path leads past the hole of the large quarry and out to the summit of Castle Crag, with wonderful views now looking down the valley, over Grange, to Keswick and Skiddaw beyond.

Retrace steps, and near the bottom of the scree slope, is the route for the short cut if required. This reduces the walk to about 5 miles, and if this is the chosen option, turn left off the path just before reaching the bottom of the quarry debris to a stile over the wall. There are two stiles just a few metres apart, but it is the higher, left one which is required. Go over the stile, and head left down the field on a grassy path through the bracken, and descend steeply to the bottom of the field, and the path then goes on steeply down through woodland to reach the river bank down in the valley.

Turn right alongside the river and follow the bank as far as the stone bridge, New Bridge. Cross over the river and turn right to continue along the bank, until turning left along a track to walk into Rosthwaite. Pass the village hall and the car park, and reach the road near the Village Store **(6)**, having rejoined the main route.

Main route, continued

Descend over the wooden stile, through the stone stile, passing the memorial to Sir William Hamer on the left, to rejoin the old pack horse route which is here part of the Allerdale Ramble. As it levels off, magnificent views open up ahead, with the distinctive whaleback of Great Gable straight ahead, and Glaramara with its rocky lumps, slightly to the left. Soon Rosthwaite can be seen down to the left, built around the small rocky lumps (*Roches moutonnées*) which are fragments of hard rock, not removed by ice erosion. About one mile ahead can be seen the gap towards which we are heading, along a more or less horizontal route, though with a few undulations.

Pass a path going left down through a wall, and our track begins to climb slightly (leading up to the old Rigghead quarries), but we can fork off left along a clear path which retains a horizontal route, whilst the original track curves up Tongue Gill. Our path crosses the stream by a wooden footbridge, followed by a smaller bridge and then a gate, to rejoin the track which has detoured up the valley. Just past the gate, the track goes down to the left, but we fork right along a path maintaining a roughly horizontal route. We go slightly up to a small wooden gate, and straight on, then across a small wooden footbridge, crossing a deep gully. There is now a wall on our left. Cross another footbridge over a deeply cut stream, and just beyond this is a ladder stile going left over a wall, which is the path to the edge of Johnny Wood, noted for ferns, lichens and damp loving plants, but we keep straight on.

As the big valley ahead comes into sight, views to the right towards Honister begin to open up, and we can also see down left towards the flat valley floor. We begin to descend, with a wall on our left, and reach two gates, right for Honister and left for Seatoller. Go left, and across the field to reach a track and turn left along this to go on downhill. Pass through a kissing gate by a large wooden gate, along a very stony track. Seatoller is down to the right, and the end of the Seathwaite valley can be seen ahead. Just beyond another gate, the track curves round to the right, between small banks, to descend to another small gate by a larger gate, and straight on down to another gate and the road. This is the bottom of Honister Pass **(4)**.

Turn left to walk through Seatoller, which is only a tiny collection of buildings, including the National Park Information centre in Seatoller Barn. This, unfortunately, only opens during the summer months, but it is packed with displays and interesting information about the locality and the weather, a very important topic in what is the wettest part of England. There is Bed and Breakfast on offer in Seatoller, and also the Yew Tree Country Restaurant, with ice creams if required.

Pass Seatoller Farm on the left, then the bus shelter, car park and toilets. Turn left through the car park and follow the stony track up to a gate, and then turn right to walk alongside the wall. At the end of the field, go through a gate in the wall, and follow the path, more or less straight on through the woodland. Moss thrives on many of the old trees and on the rocks, in this very damp environment. Down to the right is a bridge (Folly Bridge) over the stream and a gate, and a way out to the road.

Go through a gate and straight on, with woods up to the left. This is a very rocky path, as in several parts of this walk. Reach a small gate and arrive at the river bank, where we bend round to the left, across some bare rocks, which can be slippery so take great care. There is a fixed chain to hold in one place to help across the trickiest part. On the other bank can be seen an outcrop of glacier deposits, part of the tons of rock debris deposited by ice when it was melting at the end of the glacial phase. Here a large glacier coming down the Seathwaite valley and from Honister must have stopped and melted, leaving this mound of moraine which made a ridge, running across the valley from the river bank opposite along the field beyond. The ice depositing this must have stopped at this point, but in earlier times a much bigger glacier must have continued into the main Borrowdale valley, joining the Stonethwaite glacier and going on downstream to form the hollows in which Derwent Water and Bassenthwaite are situated.

The River Derwent is quite turbulent here, and can move very large rocks, as can be seen by the size of some boulders in the middle of the stream, as we move on downstream to walk past the Youth Hostel **(5)**. Shortly beyond here, do not continue along the left bank of the river, but turn right, over the stone hump bridge and walk up the narrow road. As it bends right, note the cottage on the right is called Moraine Cottage, and here we turn left through a gate along a driveway and along the right margin of a field to a gate. Then go diagonally across the next field, towards the houses, and along the right margin of the next field, with the fairly modern stone houses on the right. Beyond these houses is a small tree-covered hill, which is a *roche moutonnée*, a solid lump of rock not removed by ice erosion. As a glacier passed down the valley this harder lump was not fully eroded, the upvalley right-hand side can be seen to have a fairly gentle slope, but the left side of the hillock is much steeper. Trees grow on this rock even though the soil is very thin.

Go through the gate, on to a track and turn right for a few metres, then left along the narrow road. Wind between the delightful old stone houses of Rosthwaite and turn right to walk past Borrowdale Institute and then the car park, before reaching the main road, by the General Shop and Village Store **(6)**. Pub and hotels are to the right, but we turn left along the B5289, the main road along Borrowdale.

The flat valley floor was a lake a few thousand years ago, but was filled in by deltaic debris brought and deposited by the rivers. In more recent times, the valley has been flooded and marker posts can be seen further along the roads. Floods are less serious than they used to be, because the river channels have been dug out and embanked. Cross over a river bridge, the Stonethwaite Beck flowing to join the Derwent, and just keep going along the roadside.

The wide valley begins to narrow, and up to the left can be seen the top of Castle Crag, and over to the left can be seen the line of our route earlier in the walk. Where the valley becomes very narrow is called the Jaws of Borrowdale, where the rock was too hard for the ice to erode as rapidly as happened further up stream and also further down the valley. It is so narrow that for a long time there was no road here, the original route into Borrowdale passing through Watendlath.

As the valley narrows a damp area is on the left, with wetland trees, alder and willow, and then the river is very close to the road, and the valley sides are very steep.

Look out for a stile and a small gate across on the right, and a signpost to the Bowder Stone. Walk up the footpath to visit this huge erratic block, described by Wordsworth as: 'A mass of rock, resembling, as it lay right at the foot of that moist precipice, a stranded ship with keel upturned that rests fearless of wind and waves'.

Notice many other large stones on the slopes to the right, all the effect of frost action, whereby repeated freezing and thawing over a long time will cause the rocks to shatter. Continue along the track beyond the Bowder Stone, pass through a gate, passing a quarry where a few trees have established themselves, and reach the car park, where tree planting and landscaping have turned the old quarry site into a useful car park. One of many examples of the hand of man (often the National Trust) managing the countryside.

December

Grizedale

Partially in woodland, where views are often restricted, this walk reaches the top of Carron Fell from where all the surrounding hills can be seen. It then continues to give excellent views of Coniston, the lake, the village and the Old Man. Shelter is provided by the woodland if the day is windy and raw, and discovering sculptures in various locations adds interest to the circuit in the forest.

Length: 5 miles with a 4½ mile extension down towards Brantwood.

Time required: about 2 hours, or 4 if the full figure-of-eight walk is to be completed.

Terrain: undulating with several moderate ascents and descents. The paths are often gravelled and good for winter walking, but off the main forestry tracks it can be very damp and muddy.

Map: O.S. 1:25,000 Outdoor Leisure map number 7, the English Lakes South Eastern region. There is also a very clear map available from the Visitor Centre at Grizedale.

Starting point: GR335944, at the Visitor Centre, reached along a narrow road from Hawkshead.

Facilities: Hawkshead is the nearest town and is accessible by bus. It also contains a selection of pubs and cafes, as well as a Tourist Information Centre (015394 36525).

Weather

This was a dull and wet month in 1998, with a dominance of westerly weather – a typical December, with very changeable weather. The daily maxima temperatures were down to 1°C in the first week but rose to 13° in the second week, only to decline again before Christmas. A little snow had fallen on the hills, but white on the hills does not constitute a white Christmas for the betting fraternity, for whom snow has to fall on Christmas Day. There were several very wet days, often showing great variations within a few miles. For example on the 30th the rainfall totals for Kendal and Keswick were 10mms (0.04") and 167mm (0.68") respectively. Days with more than 247mms (one inch) were the 8th and 14th, and it this rainfall which contributes to the growth of rich forests, as at Grizedale, where the average annual rainfall over a period of years has been recorded as 1824mm (74"). Of this total, 202mm (8.2") falls in December, the second wettest month of the year (January being slightly wetter) with an average of 19 wet days. The total number of wet days in a year is 214, but many of these only record light rain. The average temperature in Grizedale in December is 2°C (height is about 100m), and so during the winter there is very little plant growth, as temperatures are well below the required 6°C. In the forest, the growing season averages about 220 days per annum, though considerable local variations are created by altitude and aspect.

Looking from Grizedale Forest over the surrounding hills

The countryside

There is little warmth in the sun at this time of year, and so the main source of warmth is from the oceans whence the westerly winds blow. From the walking point of view it is often better when cold northerly winds blow even though the temperatures will be lower, magnificent clear views can be enjoyed more than in the summer. Shorter hours of daylight are a further drawback of the winter months. The Grizedale landscape is varied, with mature trees, young trees and open recently cleared areas. Deciduous trees are bare and the Grizedale forest now has a policy of planting many deciduous trees, but the coniferous woods can provide shelter for a winter walk, and the noise of the wind can be heard whistling through the trees. Birds are not always easily seen in the forests, but they are there, with tits and goldcrests being the most likely small birds to be seen. The trees also provide winter homes and feeding territory for crossbills and winter visiting finches, including bramblings. Larger birds include the everpresent crows, who are a real success story, as they seem to thrive in all environments. The much bigger raven may also be seen, either on its own or with its mate, as they pair for life. Other larger birds include the kestrel and buzzard, likely to be seen hovering around, and the quick moving sparrowhawk darting through the trees. A larger version of the sparrowhawk in life style and hunting habits is the goshawk and there are now a few of these magnificent birds living in Grizedale. The goshawk is at the top of the food chain and will occasionally take birds as large as jays and crows. They had become extinct in the 1880s but were reintroduced in the 1960s and 1970s, and seem to be doing well in selected locations.

Wren

Forestry

The Forestry Commission was formed to produce as much timber as possible, but the modern aims are much wider, and nowhere is this shown more clearly than in Grizedale. Grizedale Forest is managed by the Forest Enterprise section of the modern Forestry Commission. Timber is produced commercially, but there is a cycle of planting in order to farm the timber as a long-term sustainable business. Also a greater variety of trees is planted including large numbers of deciduous, in order to improve the scenery and also to provide a wide range of habitats for wild life. At the visitor centre is the renowned Theatre in the Forest, with an extensive and varied programme. Also, dotted through parts of the forest are some wonderful sculptures using natural materials, and a map is available to locate the famous Forest Sculptures. As many of these have a limited life, they may be replaced, and others are added, so continuous change is taking place. Grizedale also caters for walkers, cyclists, orienteers and campers, and is a highly successful multi functional user of the land.

European Larch

Sitka Spruce

Scots Pine

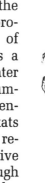

Douglas Fir

Arthur Ransome

Bank Ground Farm, seen on this walk, is thought to be the basis for Holly Howe in Ransome's most famous book "Swallows and Amazons", and much of the delightful film of this book was shot near this farm. Next to it along the road is the Lanehead Outdoor Education Centre, which may have influenced the shape and description of Beckfoot, although this was probably more influenced by Lake End at Nibthwaite, where Ransome had stayed as a child. Lanehead was owned by Miss Emma Holt, but was for a time the home of the Collingwoods who invited Ransome to stay there. W.G.Collingwood was artist, historian, Ruskin's biographer and Secretary. One of the

Collingwood's daughters, Dora, married Ernest Altounyan, a doctor, and went to live in Syria. They had 5 children and frequently returned to the Lakes for holidays – and stayed at Lanehead and later at Bank Ground. These children provided the models for the Swallows.

Brantwood

The original cottage dated from 1797, but many changes since that time turned it into a complex building. Ruskin bought the house in 1871 and it was his home from 1872 until his death in 1900. He considered the house to have the best lake and mountain views in England. During his time there the house became a noted world literary and artistic centre, and the contents now reveal much of its history and significance. Amongst his vast writing and many famous quotes, Ruskin is perhaps best known for his comment about the joy of living – "There is no wealth but life". There is the excellent Jumping Jenny restaurant at the house, worth a visit in its own right, and there are also 30 acres of hillside gardens to walk through. Outside the garden, a small nature trail around the 250 acre estate has been created, and part of this is seen on our walk, even if you do not take the diversion to visit the house and garden (for which there is an admission fee – and two hours will be required).

Morning breaks as I write, along those Coniston Fells, and the level mists, motionless, and grey beneath the rose of the moorlands, veil the lower woods, and the sleeping village, and the long lawns by the lake shore.
(John Ruskin -12th February 1878).

Anyone wishing to walk from Brantwood over to Grizedale, should follow the route of the Brantwood Nature Trail up to point number 12, which is near location number 4 on the walk described below. Just retrace this route. Alternatively, the entire circular walk could be followed, using Brantwood as the starting point, as it can be joined at either marker post 12 or marker post 13 on the Brantwood Nature Trail.

Brantwood

The Walk

From the car park **(1)** return to the road and turn right as far as the end of the buildings, then turn right to walk past the theatre. The narrow surfaced road leads to the left of Home Farm and over the small river, and where the green, yellow and red routes go straight ahead and up the slope, our route goes left through a gate. This is a public bridleway signposted to Farra Grain Gill and Satterthwaite. The stony driveway is a cycle route as well, and begins to go uphill through a grassy open area at first. The woods are up to the right, and Grizedale Beck is down to the left.

Reach a few trees and cross over a cattle grid, and the track divides with the cycle route turning right but we go ahead and slightly left, continuing along the surfaced track. The track continues through deciduous trees, with open fields down to the left, and good views to the far valley wall, which is covered with trees (including large patches of larch) right up to the top of the slope. We pass a wooden and stone structure, the first of several sculptures to be seen on this walk.

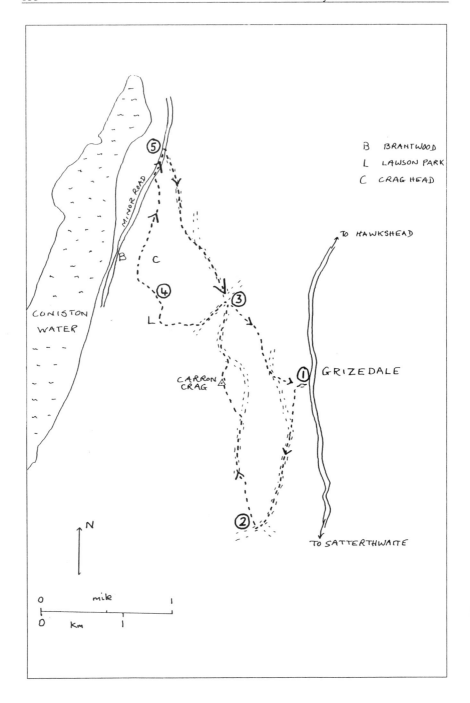

B   BRANTWOOD
L   LAWSON PARK
C   CRAG HEAD

TO HAWKSHEAD

CONISTON
WATER

GRIZEDALE

CARRON
CRAG

TO SATTERTHWAITE

N

0   mile   1

0   Km   1

Pass a track coming in from the left, and as we bend round to the right, our track divides, with the left fork dropping down into a valley (Farra Grain Gill and picnic tables), and the right fork bending round towards the right. We follow neither of these, but turn right here, off the track, to follow the path (2) going up hill into the trees, and soon passing a wooden structure with a seat. We are now on the Silurian Way, and following green markers on the posts.

The narrow path leads up through trees, mainly deciduous, beneath a wooden arch with insects carved on it, to emerge on an exposed and more open area with recent cutting and some new planting of conifers (1998). Keep going along a stony track, which soon reaches a major track where the red trail has come up from the right to join us. After 50 metres along the track, turn left through a large deer proof gate, and climb up through the conifers. We are now following red and green markers on the posts. This leads us to the triangulation point on the top of Carron Fell (1029ft – 314m), with good views back over rolling hills covered in trees, mainly evergreen and larch, with the green fields down in the valley, and a few white houses in Satterthwaite. Away to the west is the Old Man of Coniston.

Follow the red and green marker posts down from the summit, and views to the valley and road can be seen. At the large gate and fence, emerge on to the main track again and turn left. Ignore a left turn off our track, and keep looking out for the small sculptures, one with a nuthatch coming down the carving and then a butterfly. A well-grown wood is on the left, but on the right clearance took place in 1998. This highlights a problem of route finding in these forests, as their appearance changes from one year to the next. Planting changes and when I walked this route early in 1998 there was forest on both sides, but by the end of the year the forest on the right had been removed. By now (whenever you are reading this) new trees are likely to have been planted. The track continues to descend from Carron Fell, and just before it begins to climb a little and bend to the left, the green and red routes turn sharp right. If going on the full route, notice this right turn for future reference.

We either turn right here, for the shorter route, or keep ahead for the longer route, for an extra 4½ miles (2 hours) via Brantwood and the Coniston valley.

But for the short cut, to return to the Grizedale Centre, turn right following red and green rings on the posts, and descend along a broad path, passing a new area of Sculptures, an international Sculpture Trail created from 1998. Continue on down, to reach a major track where we are joined by the yellow route as well. Turn right here and continue until reaching the path going left, where the yellow, red and green routes all descend to Home Farm and back to the starting point.

Longer route

Beyond the sharp right turn, the short cut route, after another 50m the track splits (3) and we turn left here, to walk a circuit down towards Coniston and Brantwood, but ending this circuit coming along the track which is the right fork here.

Having turned left, past a very windy corner where trees have been showing the effects of wind damage – uprooted trees seen here or elsewhere will show how thin the soil is. Walk along a level stretch, and then as the track begins to slope down, look for a path off to the right, with a public bridleway sign. (The green cycleway sign points straight ahead) Go steadily downhill, through the forest (I suppose this could all be cleared by the time you read this), to be joined by a path coming in from the left. Continue on down to the edge of the woods, where views of Coniston Old Man and Coniston Water open up. Cross a track coming down from the right, and continuing to the left, passing the buildings of Lawsons. This old farm is mentioned in "Plague Dogs" by Richard Adams.

Our path goes straight ahead, with Lawsons to the left, and we reach a gate, where we leave Forest Enterprise land and move on to Brantwood Estate (4). Just follow the gravel path going downhill, to reach an iron gate, then cross a stream and reach a Marker Post, number 12. This is on a numbered walk from Brantwood, coming up from the left to join the path we are on. Walk alongside the stone wall to our left, to reach post number 13, where a stone staircase goes up to the right. This is the Brantwood Estate Walk up to the summit of Crag Head, passing points 14, 15, 16, 17 – but we go straight ahead.

Reach an S-shaped seat, with a wooden back and bench on stone foundations, and then we begin to descend, and reach post 18. The Brantwood path comes down from the right here, and goes through the wall on the left. Anyone wishing to visit Brantwood must walk down to the house and pay the admission fee for the garden, and the house too if you have enough time.

Keep straight on, cross a stream and then curve left, and descend to a wooden gate. Beyond this, go on down through the trees, mixed deciduous, including some huge old beech, to reach a gate and the road. Opposite is the driveway to Low Bank Ground, an Outdoor Education Centre. We turn right along the road **(5)**, passing Bank Ground Farm with a Ransome Society notice Board telling us that this is Holly Howe, and Kanchenjunga is across the lake. As the road begins to bend left, turn right at the white buildings of Lanehead, where a bridleway sign points to the right.

Turn right at Lanehead, up the stony track, with an old stone barn on our left. Soon reach a gate, beyond which the track splits, left to Esthwaite and right to Satterthwaite and Grizedale. We turn right, along a very rocky path, often with water running down it, which is true of many locations in the Lake District, where many paths provide easy routes for flowing water after rain has been falling. Keep straight ahead along the track, then bend left and then right to cross over a stream (Black Beck). We are passing through a mainly deciduous area, which can be very colourful in autumn. Reach a gate with a stile alongside, and go on into the woods, passing a few log barriers on the path, used to drain water off the path, instead of rocks which are more usual. The stony track passes through an area of heather and bilberry, to reach a Forestry Commission notice "Take Care: Do not start Fire", just beyond which we are joined by a clear track coming in from the left. Soon reach a larger track where we turn right, following the orange and blue cycle track signs on a marker post. Up to our left can be seen the mast on the hill top.

A path goes off to the left but we continue along the track, passing some recent planting on the left, where some deciduous are mixed in with the conifers, and a major track goes off to the left. After a further 30 metres the track splits and you may recognise this as we have been here before **(3)**. The Blue cycle route goes right and the orange goes left.

We go left here, and this track splits after a few more metres, with the Orange cycle route going right, towards Carron Fell, but we fork left and we are now on the route of the short cut described earlier, following red and green rings on the posts.

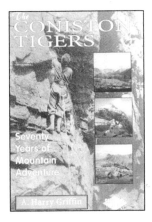

Also of interest:

THE CONISTON TIGERS: SEVENTY YEARS OF MOUNTAIN ADVENTURE

This book is the lifestory of A Harry Griffin MBE, much loved as Country Diary writer for *The Guardian*. The focus of the book is the story of Harry's rock climbing years with The Coniston Tigers club - one of the first climbing clubs in the Lake District. It is an illuminating account of climbing in its earliest days, and features many incredible period photographs of the climbers with their minimal climbing gear - some nonchalantly smoking their pipes as they balance on the most delicate ledge. Although of great interest to present-day climbers, it is a fascinating read for anyone interested in mountaineering, the outdoors, or the history of the Lake District. Harry's descriptions of the area before tourism - when the area was still a lonely, quiet place - make fascinating reading.

£14.95 (hardback)

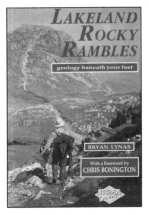

LAKELAND ROCKY RAMBLES: GEOLOGY BENEATH YOUR FEET

This is the companion book to Snowdonia Rocky Rambles: the perfect way to learn about why things look the way they do. "Refreshing ... Ambitious ... Informative ... Inspiring" NEW SCIENTIST. £9.95

TOWNS AND VILLAGES OF BRITAIN: Cumbria

Those interested in local history will find themselves thoroughly absorbed in this comprehensive gazeteer of the folklore and history of almost 300 Cumbrian towns and villages. Learn about the complex of stone circles and cairn-circle at Ainstable, the holy Well at Humphrey Head, and of brutal Scottish raiders on the borderlands.

"fascinating facts about almost every place on the county map...any Cumbrians interested in their locality will appreciate an opportunity to read this book" CUMBERLAND & WESTMORLAND HERALD

£8.95

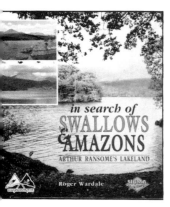

100 LAKE DISTRICT WALKS
If you plan to buy just one book of Lakeland walks, this is the one you need: "A useful addition to any walker's library" WEST CUMBERLAND GAZETTE. £7.95

IN SEARCH OF SWALLOWS & AMAZONS:
Arthur Ransome's Lakeland
This is a new edition of a popular book originally published in 1986. Additional material has been added to satisfy even the most avid reader of "Swallows & Amazons" - three decades of Ransome hunting with text and photographs to identify the locations of the ever-popular series of books. There's a two fold pleasure in this book - enjoying the original stories and discovering the farms, rivers, islands, towns and hills that formed their backdrop. £7.95

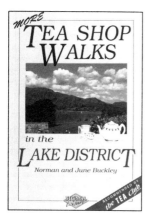

TEA SHOP WALKS IN THE LAKE DISTRICT
The original – now in its second edition! Do not confuse with any other book misleadingly using the same title! Scones with strawberry jam and other delights await weary walkers. A leisurely introduction to the Lake District. £6.95

MORE TEA SHOP WALKS IN THE LAKE DISTRICT
Norman and June Buckley have planned more leisurely rambles in this companion volume to the first tea shop book on the region. Crossing both the central regions and the lesser-known fringe areas, their 25 easy-going, circular walks range from 2 to 9 miles. £6.95

WALKS IN MYSTERIOUS NORTH LAKELAND
An unusual collection of 30 walks which provide a unique opportunity to visit places with a strange and mythical history.
"Each walk features remarkable hand-drawn maps and stylish, entertaining writing that is almost as good to read before a roaring open fire as on the open fells" LAKELAND WALKER.
'Graham writes with robust enthusiasm...colourful excursions' KESWICK REMINDER. £6.95

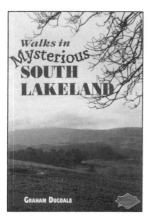

WALKS IN MYSTERIOUS SOUTH LAKELAND

Old Nick, witches, wizards, monsters, fairies, and grizzly monsters! Graham Dugdale intertwines intriguing tales of these dark beings with his 30 skilfully chosen gentle walks in south Cumbria. "This is a well-researched guide book, well written, with a welcome thread of humour." THE GREAT OUTDOORS. *£6.95*

BEST PUB WALKS IN THE LAKE DISTRICT

This, the longest-established (and best-researched) pub walks book for the Lakes, is amazingly wide-ranging, with an emphasis on quality of walks and the real ale rewards that follow! *£6.95*

LAKELAND WALKING: ON THE LEVEL

Walk among the highest mountains of Lakeland and avoid the steep ascents - with no compromises on the views! "A good spread of walks" RAMBLING TODAY. *£6.95*

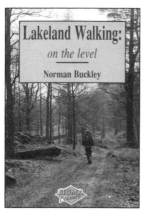

MOSTLY DOWNHILL: Leisurely Walks in the Lake District

Yes, this minor miracle is possible - if you cheat slightly and take a car or bus to the start of the walk! "Perfect companion; thoroughly recommended" MENCAP NEWS. *£6.95*

SOUTH LAKELAND WALKS WITH CHILDREN

South Lakeland offers some spectacular walking country, with gentle fells, good tourist amenities, panoramic views - and plenty to amuse children. The twenty circular walks in this volume are spread across the whole of the Southern Lakes and all are written with children in mind. Each walk includes easy-to-follow directions (for mums and dads) with instructions on where to point out interesting things that will fascinate young walkers - everything from fir cones to wild flowers, church spires to squirrels. Some routes are suitable for pushchairs and these are clearly identified. All are on well-maintained paths that are easily negotiated by little people. *£6.95*

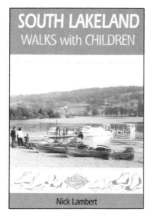

BEST PUB WALKS ON THE LAKELAND FRINGES

The fringes of the Lake District have a great atmosphere of peace - a quality which has almost vanished from the crowded central areas of England's favourite National Park. In this collection of 25 walks, Neil Coates takes a fresh approach to the area, urging ramblers to abandon the crowds and discover the tranquility of the mountain paths, wild woodland, waterfalls and local heritage of the Lake District Fringes. Walks range from 4 to 11 miles and each one features a refreshing stop at a quiet village pub or country inn, personally selected by the author. £6.95

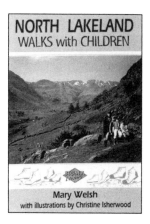

NORTH LAKELAND WALKS WITH CHILDREN

This book contains walks for all ages - none too long - even for the youngest of ramblers. The author points out plants, birds and animals along the route and gives details of historical and industrial artefacts. She poses questions of interest for all the family, many of which are illustrated by Christine Isherwood's delightful pen and ink drawings. *£6.95*

All of our books are available through booksellers. In case of difficulty, or for a free catalogue, please contact: **SIGMA LEISURE, 1 SOUTH OAK LANE, WILMSLOW, CHESHIRE SK9 6AR.**
Phone: 01625-531035
Fax: 01625-536800.
E-mail: sigma.press@zetnet.co.uk .
Web site: http//www.sigmapress.co.uk
MASTERCARD and VISA orders welcome. Please add £2 p&p to all orders.